Bev Aisbett is the author and illustrator of several highly regarded self-help texts for sufferers of anxiety and depression, most notably *Living with IT* and *Taming the Black Dog*. These books are distributed to health professionals nationwide and have been translated into four languages.

A trained counsellor, Bev is also the facilitator of the Art of Anxiety recovery program in Melbourne. For those unable to attend her workshop in person, she offers a home-study version, *The Art of Anxiety DVD Workshop*, as well as other online resources and services. She conducts lectures to assist sufferers of depression and anxiety within metropolitan and regional Victoria.

Bev is also a recognised artist, and her soulful paintings have been regularly exhibited in Victoria and Tasmania.

Workshop and lecture information,
and other anxiety resources:
www.bevaisbettartofanxiety.com

BY BEV AISBETT

Living IT Up

Letting IT Go

Get Real

Taming the Black Dog

The Little Book of IT

Fixing IT

Recovery: A Journey to Healing

The Book of IT

Get Over IT

I Love Me

All of IT: A Memoir

Living with IT

30 Days 30 Ways to Overcome Anxiety

30 Days 30 Ways to Overcome Depression

30 DAYS 30 WAYS

TO OVERCOME DEPRESSION

BEV AISBETT

HarperCollins*Publishers*

HarperCollins*Publishers*

First published in Australia in 2020
by HarperCollins*Publishers* Australia Pty Limited
ABN 36 009 913 517
harpercollins.com.au

HarperCollins*Publishers*
Level 13, 201 Elizabeth Street, Sydney NSW 2000, Australia
Unit D1, 63 Apollo Drive, Rosedale, Auckland 0632, New Zealand
A 53, Sector 57, Noida, UP, India
1 London Bridge Street, London, SE1 9GF, United Kingdom
Bay Adelaide Centre, East Tower, 22 Adelaide Street West, 41st floor,
   Toronto, Ontario M5H 4E3, Canada
195 Broadway, New York NY 10007, USA

ISBN: 978 1 4607 5810 6 (pbk)
ISBN: 978 1 4607 1185 9 (ebook)
ISBN: 978 1 4607 8029 9 (audio book)

Front cover and internal illustrations by Bev Aisbett
Cover design by Hazel Lam, HarperCollins Design Studio
Typeset in Brandon Grotesque by Kelli Lonergan
Printed and bound in Australia by McPhersons Printing Group
The papers used by HarperCollins in the manufacture of this book are a natural,
recyclable product made from wood grown in sustainable plantation forests. The fibre
source and manufacturing processes meet recognised international environmental
standards, and carry certification.

DEDICATION

To Sri Parvati Sundari –
for so much

INTRODUCTION

All of my books are written through LIVED EXPERIENCE, so I know you're hurting and how bad you feel. I've been there and I know the dark hole of depression is a HORRIBLE place to find yourself.

It may surprise you to know that I still make the occasional (but rare) return visit to that dark hole when the going gets tough.

But not for LONG and not too DEEPLY. Now I know BETTER and that's what I'm handing on to you in this book – the things that have turned my visits into quick DROP-INS, rather than long PRISON SENTENCES.

I'm not always going to go easy on you, quite simply because patting your hand isn't going to HELP.

All the sympathy in the world isn't going to motivate you to MOVE ON. I'm not going to invest ONE MINUTE in your disempowerment. I'm not going to tell you you're a VICTIM, because then you'll start believing you are. I'm going to call on you to step up and out of this darkness because you CAN. And I believe that you got yourself into this big, dark hole because it was the only thing you knew how to do in response to STRESS, LOSS or HURT.

Those old responses of retreat, shutdown and numbness that once PROTECTED you are now not only UNHELPFUL and INEFFECTIVE, but they are also doing you HARM. It's time to find a different way of managing the tough things that come along with life, instead of going into COLLAPSE.

Now, I'm assuming that if you've picked up this book it means that you're finally fed up with being in this hole and are ready to move on. Or it may be that someone has plonked this book down in front of you because THEY'RE fed up and want you to move on.

Either way, it's time for you to start climbing, and if you're ready to give it your best shot and put in a bit of work on yourself, this book will guide you on that climb.

You can do the 30 Days any way you like – as DAILY exercises or WEEKLY or MONTHLY – it's up to you. You can even go back and repeat days if you want to. All you'll need is a pen and paper, and an open mind.

One thing I ask is this: once you've started, KEEP GOING. Make that commitment to yourself – because you DON'T DESERVE to feel this lousy and you really don't NEED to.

So, are you ready? Good. Let's get CRACKING!

DAY 1

You're right – life can seriously SUCK at times

Yep – life is no walk in the park. It's not EASY, it's not SMOOTH; it doesn't unfold all NEAT and TIDY like a Hollywood movie.

There are times when life slams you HARD. There are times when your heart BREAKS.

And if you've picked up this book, I suspect you're going through (or have gone through) at least one of these times.

I HEAR YOU. I GET IT.

You could tell me your story and it would have the same title as every other story of depression – 'It's Not Fair.'

Well, here's the thing. Nobody ever carved in stone 'Life will be FAIR'. Despite this, at the heart of our disappointments and sorrows is the idea that life SHOULD be fair and that unfair things should not happen to us. And yet they DO.

If there is one ABSOLUTE in life, it is this: you WILL be challenged! However, how MUCH you are AFFECTED by these challenges is actually very much in your hands.

The first thing we need to dispose of is the idea of a 'rewards' system – i.e., if I do good things, I'll be rewarded; or bad things only happen to me because I'm a 'bad' person or I've 'failed' in some way.

And life should punish those I deem to be bad or unworthy, and life is unjust if they get to walk away without consequence.

The notion that life is some sort of sideshow alley – where you win the teddy bear for the number of goodness points earned, or the booby prize when you don't meet the quota – is one that keeps you in misery when things don't turn out the way you would like.

Life ISN'T fair when it's limited to your EXPECTATIONS. How can it be, when what might seem FAIR to you, seems UNFAIR to someone else? What seems WRONG to you may be perfectly REASONABLE to someone else.

The truth is, life is neither FAIR nor UNFAIR – it just IS.

We tend to impose HUMAN TRAITS on anything from animals to cars or even the weather – as though they have a will and CHOOSE not to do what we WANT them to do.

But does the river have a personal AGENDA to flood your house?

No – the river is just doing its THING and your house happened to be in its WAY. You might have even built your house on a FLOOD PLAIN!

And your life has been like that – things have come along and you were in the WAY of them. No matter what opinion you place upon such events – RIGHT or WRONG, FAIR or UNFAIR – they HAPPENED. And they happened to you simply because you were THERE.

Life is just rolling along like a big river, and you're either going to insist on paddling AGAINST THE TIDE (because that would be FAIR!) or go WITH the way the CURRENT is flowing.

There IS a way to navigate life so that you don't end up dashed against the rocks each time there's a challenge (and this book will help STEER you); but just for now, if it makes you feel any better, I'll AGREE with you: yes, sometimes life seems to truly SUCK. So be it.

WORKING DAY I

- Today, try to embrace the idea that life is neither FAIR nor UNFAIR. Also, let go of the idea you are being REWARDED or PUNISHED.

- On a piece of paper, write down the event or situation that you feel MOST DEPRESSED about. Next, draw a series of squares (about six squares should be enough) to represent a row of doors. Number each door.

  Behind DOOR 1 is the choice (or choices) you made in response to the event you listed.

  Clearly, your FIRST choice was to BECOME DEPRESSED.

  Now go to DOOR 2. Behind this door is a DIFFERENT choice you could have made in the way that you responded to the situation. What ELSE could you have done, besides getting DEPRESSED? Behind each door is ANOTHER POSSIBILITY.

  See how many different choices you can reveal.

- How have you put yourself IN the way of things that have happened? Reflect on how you could have moved OUT of the way instead.

YOUR
MANTRAS
FOR
DAY 1

*'Today, I will accept my life
as it IS and WAS,
not as I think it SHOULD be
or SHOULD HAVE been.'*

*'What if I stopped taking
life so PERSONALLY?'*

DAY 2

You're not Robinson Crusoe

You might feel as though you're going through a UNIQUE experience that nobody else can possibly understand; however, depression is actually a very COMMON human experience.

Most people will experience feelings of depression at some time in their lives, usually following a LIFE CHANGE or LOSS.

In fact, there are 300 MILLION people who have been diagnosed with depression worldwide.

However, statistics can be MISLEADING – the above figure includes people who have PASSING depression (as a result of a life crisis), and this figure does not include the OUTCOME for people who have had depression.

Given that there are about 7.7 BILLION people on the planet, that leaves a lot of people who are simply going about their normal lives without any great, dark cloud hovering over them.

In fact, some people actually ENJOY life – now, there's a CONCEPT! And there are even some people who have been where you are, who have thrown off their dark cloud and found that life can again be SATISFYING, INTERESTING and PLEASURABLE – despite being full of CHALLENGES and CONTRASTS, as it has ALWAYS been.

So, what might these people be doing that you're not?

Let's take a look.

> They're nice to themselves
> They've found something to love
> They have something to do
> They take life as it is
> They've moved on from the past
> They've focused their mind on thoughts
> that support them

While all this might seem out of reach from where you currently are, it is POSSIBLE to feel better. It takes a COMMITMENT to do so, and that means making FEELING BETTER a PRIORITY.

The ONLY difference between those who aren't in your emotional place and YOU is that you're not doing the things that make you feel BETTER (including and ESPECIALLY helpful THINKING) and they ARE.

You are not being asked to FLY TO MARS or GROW AN EXTRA LEG or CURE CANCER; you are simply being asked to take a good, hard look at how YOU make life HARD for yourself and DO SOMETHING ELSE.

WORKING DAY 2

- Recognise that EVERYBODY gets down sometimes.

- I hate to tell you but you're not that IMPORTANT! No-one is scrutinising or judging your EVERY MOVE. You're SPECIAL – but you're not THAT special!

- Likewise, you have not been SINGLED OUT by the universe for SUFFERING!

- Consider the QUALITIES of people who feel good about themselves and enjoy life. How might you adopt these same qualities?

YOUR
MANTRA
FOR
DAY 2

*'We're all doing the BEST we can
with what we KNOW at the time.'*

DAY 3

Shame, Shame, SHAME

'You BLEW IT! You got it ALL WRONG!'

'You're HOPELESS! You don't DESERVE to be HAPPY! You don't deserve to be LOVED!'

'What an IDIOT! Only a FOOL would mess up their lives so COMPLETELY. Who would want someone as MESSED UP as you?'

'Oh well, you've ruined EVERYTHING now, haven't you? May as well call it QUITS.'

Now, isn't that INTERESTING? I can hear what you're thinking right now:

'Wow, she's being really RUDE and MEAN to me!'

'Talk about kicking someone when they're DOWN!'

'She has no right to DISRESPECT me like this! Who does she think she is?'

Or are you instead saying to yourself:

'Gee, it wasn't quite THAT bad. I mean, I TRIED. I did my BEST and some things turned out okay!'

See what I just DID? I just showed you how you TREAT YOURSELF!

It doesn't feel GOOD to have someone ELSE say it to you, does it?

Well, I have NEWS for you: it doesn't feel good to hear it from YOURSELF, either!

And did you notice that you actually started to DEFEND yourself when I 'attacked' you?

So, what's going on here?

Well, (a) you're BULLYING yourself, aren't you?

And (b) maybe you're exaggerating just a little how much DAMAGE you've actually done.

And (c) maybe, just maybe, things (including you) are not quite as BAD as they SEEM.

In any case, it's not FUN to be on the RECEIVING end of criticism and endlessly negative messages, is it? Maybe that has something to do with why you feel so BAD! Perhaps you need to GIVE YOURSELF A BREAK! You did all you KNEW to do. You did the BEST you could.

WORKING DAY 3

- Today, NOTICE all your mental criticisms of yourself and your life.

  Write them down. Now imagine that SOMEONE ELSE is levelling these criticisms at you. Would you ACCEPT these as true without question?

- List every name you have ever been called. This list includes TITLES, PET NAMES, NICKNAMES, TERMS OF ENDEARMENT and NASTY NAMES (for want of a better word).

  Read the list out loud. Notice the WARMTH that you feel with the terms of endearment and the PAIN you feel with the nasty names.

- Okay, now list every name YOU HAVE CALLED YOURSELF. Read them out.

  Consider this: which names have done the most DAMAGE – the names you were called by OTHERS or the names you have called YOURSELF?

YOUR MANTRAS FOR DAY 3

'I am a HUMAN BEING. I make MISTAKES.'

'It is through mistakes that I LEARN.'

'I do not deserve to be BULLIED for making mistakes while I learn.'

DAY 4

But THEY did this to ME

One thing that is INEVITABLE in life is that, sooner or later, you're going to feel HURT by something SOMEONE ELSE has done.

You may feel:

Let down

Abandoned

Cheated

Criticised

Overlooked

Unloved

Abused

If you have depression, it's a strong bet that you associate its onset with someone else's less-than-desirable behaviour towards you.

Indeed, you may have been subjected to what could be described as CRUELTY, and this has led you to feel UNLOVED, UNWORTHY and UNTRUSTING.

While this is a BIG subject and one that you may need some ongoing therapy to fully work through, today we're going to do a little basic GROUNDWORK on how to see this from a HEALTHIER PERSPECTIVE.

So to begin with, let's look at that SOMEONE ELSE's behaviour.

The basic understandings here are:

> *People who hurt others are hurt people*
> *People who are afraid lash out*
> *People who are cruel are wounded children*
> *(even when they are adults)*

So, here's the QUESTION: why would you let the behaviour of someone who is UNEVOLVED ruin YOUR life?

The solution here is not to change someone else's behaviour but to become BIG enough yourself, to NOT TAKE IT ON. Your job is not to fix THEM. Your job is to fix YOU. And that means being fully RESPONSIBLE for your OWN wellbeing. No-one can MAKE you depressed but YOU. No-one has control over your FEELINGS but YOU.

And now, we need to take a look at YOUR part in the process and how to CHANGE that, because it's always a dance between TWO people when things go wrong.

Think of relationships as joint BANK ACCOUNTS. There are DEPOSITS and WITHDRAWALS. If the relationship is healthy, there will be an equal number of deposits and withdrawals made by both parties, so that the BALANCE remains stable.

If you feel you have been RIPPED OFF, LET DOWN, BETRAYED or ABANDONED, think of how you may have INVESTED more than you could AFFORD.

If you were looking after yourself, you would never give away so much that you were left DEPLETED.

If someone is DRAINING your account and you keep TOPPING it up, WHO is responsible for that?

If someone TAKES from you, they do so out of fear that they'll never HAVE enough.

If you OVERINVEST, it's because you fear you'll never BE enough.

It is YOUR responsibility to keep an eye on your emotional bank account. Give it all away and you'll be BROKE. Let the other person TAKE too much and the reserves will run dry.

WORKING DAY 4

- If someone has 'taken' from you, think of ways that you have INVESTED in this dynamic by giving more than you can AFFORD.

   Here are a few ways that this can happen:

   I trusted someone untrustworthy

   I didn't set clear boundaries

   I didn't say 'no' when I needed to

   I gave it one too many chances

   I was afraid that if I didn't give they wouldn't love me

   I didn't value myself

- How might you make yourself BIG enough not to be bothered by someone else's SMALLNESS?

- Now think of some ways that you can keep your own emotional bank account FILLED UP.

   Some of these might include:

   Being nicer to myself

   Setting clear boundaries

   Saying no when I need to

   Doing things I enjoy

   Being more selective in my relationships

YOUR MANTRA FOR DAY 4

'I will only give away that which I can LIVE WITHOUT.'

DAY 5

Do
some
ARITHMETIC

While we're on the subject of figures, it is said that a trouble SHARED is a trouble HALVED. You can actively REDUCE or AMPLIFY the intensity of your experience of depression by how much energy you feed it and whether that energy is directed AWAY FROM or TOWARDS it.

If you've been keeping your depression a big, dark SECRET, it's time that you told someone about it.

Why? Because it's hard to gain PERSPECTIVE from INSIDE the problem – everything looks bleak and hopeless from WITHIN depression. You think that's the way life is, but your VIEW on reality is skewed by the way you FEEL.

You also need some SUPPORT when you are feeling depressed. EVERYONE needs a little help sometimes, and here's something you may not realise: people LOVE to be NEEDED! It can feel like a real HONOUR to be the one that someone confides in. It says that you TRUST this person enough to share part of yourself.

Speaking up about the problem is also a form of RELEASE. Suddenly that heavy weight on your heart is lighter and less overwhelming because someone is HELPING you CARRY it. And here's another revelation: you will probably find that, instead of your being JUDGED, the person you're confiding in may even have their OWN experience of depression and will be able to

RELATE to yours. People are generally more GENEROUS and willing to HELP than you may believe at this point.

However, be SELECTIVE in your choice of confidant. If you know that someone loves to broadcast every aspect of their and others' lives on social media, they are NOT a good choice for you!

It may be that, instead of turning to a friend, family member or trusted colleague, you could speak to someone NEUTRAL, such as a PROFESSIONAL, or join a SUPPORT GROUP. You'll find that there are plenty of people willing to listen out there if you look around.

Okay, so that's the 'divide' part of this equation, the SHARING of your problem. What about the 'multiplication'?

Want to FEED a problem? Keep FOCUSING on it! Want to make it even BIGGER? Get a whole gang of people focusing on it!

If you are someone who does nothing but talk about how MISERABLE you are, now is the time to put a LID on it and shift your attention to something HEALTHIER.

Keeping your depression CENTRE STAGE is going to make it terribly 'important', which does nothing but feed your sense of HELPLESSNESS.

It's time to move it to the BACKGROUND. There are tips on the next page on how to do this.

WORKING DAY 5

DIVISION:

- If you haven't spoken up, now is the day to do so. Don't put it off any longer. You'll find there's nothing to be ASHAMED of after all.

  Here are some OPTIONS when seeking a CONFIDANT:

    > A trustworthy and discreet friend
    > or family member
    > A GP or therapist
    > A support group

- Keep in mind that not everyone is a natural counsellor and will know what to SAY or DO. Some people may be BETTER at handling your distress than others. Don't think you've made a MISTAKE in telling them. Just move on to a more suitable 'someone who "gets" you'.

MULTIPLICATION:

- If all you do is talk about how MISERABLE you feel, today is the day to PUT A LID ON IT!

- Today, take a holiday from all news, newspapers or social media. Also avoid dark or depressing books, movies or television, AND depressing PEOPLE!

- Also keep clear of any HEAVY or DEPRESSING CONVERSATIONS. Instead, talk to people about PLEASANT things. Ask them about the things that they ENJOY – such as their children, pets or hobbies.

- See how LIGHT you can make this day by turning your attention away from DARK and HEAVY subjects. Notice how you FEEL as a result.

YOUR
MANTRAS
FOR
DAY 5

'Too much of anything is TOO MUCH.'

'Too little of anything is TOO LITTLE.'

DAY 6

A BEAR
goes into
a CAVE

What if your mind and body knew EXACTLY what they were doing by making you feel depressed? What if there was WISDOM in this retreat from the world?

When you're depressed you don't feel like doing ANYTHING, do you? ENGAGING with people is too hard, being CHEERFUL is out of reach.

'I SHOULDN'T feel this way' is the first thing that comes to mind. 'I SHOULD be out there, doing things.'

But SHOULD you? WHY should you? Because OTHERS think you should? You don't FEEL like it, so why do it?

Right now, you can't see the forest for the trees. If you keep PUSHING against yourself, you're just going over the same old tracks and probably making them DEEPER.

Phonetically, *depressed* can also sound like *deep rest*.

When winter comes, a bear instinctively shuts up shop and heads into its CAVE.

If you keep PUSHING, STRUGGLING, FIGHTING and RESISTING, something's gotta give. And when something HAS given, give it a REST. Go into your cave – without GUILT.

Forget trying to ACHIEVE anything. That's not the point. Just GO WITH IT. Stop TRYING to be other than WHERE YOU ARE NOW.

Fighting AGAINST where you are is the TRUE source of your PAIN. ACCEPT that this is how things are AT THE MOMENT. You're more likely to resurface sooner if you ACKNOWLEDGE and ALLOW your feelings than if you think of them as being WRONG and try to BANISH them.

This day gives you permission to 'hibernate' to clear the way for the HEALING WORK ahead.

WORKING DAY 6

- Set aside this day for DEEP REST. Let everything else go. Let your body and mind RESET. This is how your SPIRIT is replenished.

- Today, attend to all your PHYSICAL needs IMMEDIATELY. If you need to SLEEP, sleep. If you're HUNGRY, eat. If you need to go to the bathroom, don't put it off till later. Get used to tuning in and listening to your body and acting on its needs IN THE MOMENT. Then it won't have to SCREAM at you to get your attention.

- Let go of any attempts to SOLVE anything today. Nothing needs to be done. Let go of TRYING. Let go of JUDGING. Let go of THINKING too much. Just BE.

- Observe yourself just being AS YOU ARE, without JUDGEMENT.

YOUR MANTRA FOR DAY 6

'Giving IN is not the same as giving UP.'

DAY 7

All is NOT as it SEEMS

Everything seems WRONG. Everything seems HOPELESS. But is it really?

The fact that you FEEL depressed doesn't necessarily mean that there IS something to be depressed about!

However, your mind will go searching for EVIDENCE to support the beliefs you hold and the MEANING you give to the things you are focused on.

What if this idea that you have attached to – that all is WRONG – doesn't actually mean anything beyond the fact that you feel OUT OF SORTS?

You can feel down as a result of many fairly innocuous things, including:

> *Becoming unwell*
> *Not getting enough sleep*
> *Eating the wrong foods*
> *Drinking alcohol*
> *Taking certain medications*

FEELING depressed doesn't mean that the world IS a mess, that there's no POINT to anything, or that you and your life are HOPELESS.

Feeling depressed simply means that you FEEL DEPRESSED.

Thoughts are not FACTS – they are OPINIONS. And with depression, the world is experienced through a DARK FILTER. This doesn't mean that there is nothing GOOD out there for you; it means that, because you are looking through that FILTER, you can't SEE anything good.

It is important that you don't confuse your depressed thinking as being EVIDENCE that everything is wrong. It ISN'T. There are only SITUATIONS you choose to focus on in a certain way, bringing to them your OPINION and, as a result, EXPERIENCING them in accordance with your opinion.

In other words, you're not seeing 'REALITY'; you're seeing your STATE OF MIND!

You can TRANSFORM a 'bad' day into a 'good' (or better) day by changing the way you 'report' the day to yourself.

Change your OPINION and EVERYTHING changes – including, and especially, how you FEEL!

WORKING DAY 7

- Notice how you 'report' events and encounters to yourself when you are feeling DEPRESSED.

- Today, simply CHANGE YOUR OPINION of these events and experiences as an experiment in how this affects your mood.

- It is important that you aim for opinions that you can INVEST IN and BELIEVE from where you are. For instance, going for 'Everything is wonderful' at this point is not going to fly. However, a more MODERATE statement, such as 'Things may not actually be as BAD as I think', may be in reach.

- Today, look for and note at least five small POSITIVE things that you may have been BLIND to because you were looking through the DARK FILTER.

YOUR
MANTRA
FOR
DAY 7

'I may THINK it, but that doesn't PROVE it.'

DAY 8

No
EXCUSES

At some stage in this 30 Days, either TODAY or NEXT WEEK or THROUGHOUT the 30 Days, you're going to tell yourself that this WON'T WORK, that you're STUCK and that you'll be depressed for the REST OF YOUR LIFE.

One of the main reasons why people get stuck in a hole is that they keep coming up with REASONS to STAY STUCK in the hole!

In other words, they keep ARGUING for their LIMITATIONS, instead of actually DOING something about them!

We use those justifications in a multitude of ways to:

> *Drink alcohol*
>
> *Use drugs*
>
> *Overeat*
>
> *Have unhealthy relationships*
>
> *Shop obsessively*
>
> *Not go out*
>
> *Not engage with people*
>
> *Stay angry, bitter and hurt*

All these excuses do is keep you locked into a TOXIC CYCLE, tethered to what is no longer even HAPPENING.

There is one reason, and one reason only, why you can't move on – you don't BELIEVE that you can.

But you are BIGGER than this. Step into your potential. No more excuses for living SMALL.

Decide that you deserve better, then your suffering will be converted from a WASTE to a MOTIVATION.

Here are some of the ARGUMENTS for LIMITATION that may be keeping you STUCK:

- 'It's a chemical imbalance.'

  The jury is still out on which comes FIRST – the CHEMICAL IMBALANCE or the STRESS (governed by thinking) that causes chemical imbalance. If you drive a car over a crack in the road often enough it will become a RUT. Likewise, if your thoughts have been running in a depressive track for long enough you will certainly cause changes in your PHYSIOLOGY.

- 'It's hereditary.'

  Is it? Or have you LEARNED how to be depressed by observation and exposure to people who are depressed?

- 'I've had a hard life.'

If so, you are in illustrious company:

>*Albert Einstein didn't speak until he was four years old*
>
>*Jim Carrey used to be homeless*
>
>*Oprah Winfrey was sexually abused as a child*
>
>*Richard Branson has dyslexia*
>
>*Stephen King's first novel was rejected 30 times*
>
>*Charlize Theron witnessed her mother kill her father*
>
>*Johnny Depp lived in more than 20 locations as a child*
>
>*Walt Disney was fired from his first job because he 'lacked imagination'*
>
>*And the list goes on ...*

In fact, most INFLUENTIAL PEOPLE have had tough beginnings and have had to strive HARD to overcome early difficulties. You don't get WISE by living a 'safe' life. They have used their trials as MOTIVATION.

- 'I lost a loved one.'

   Yes, this can be very painful, but the truth is we ALL will at some time in life. The circumstances and timing may vary, but DEATH is part of LIFE. And there will *NEVER be a good time for it to happen.* While it is HEALTHY and NECESSARY to grieve, it is not HEALTHY nor HELPFUL to be CONSUMED by loss.

- 'I lost my job.'

  Difficult, but not IMPOSSIBLE to get another. You got *this* job, didn't you?

On deeper investigation, depression – rather than being an ORGANIC disease – can in many cases be attributed to SITUATIONAL CAUSES, such as:

> *The death of someone close to you*
> *The onset of illness/disability*
> *The end of a relationship*
> *Childhood trauma*
> *Adult trauma*
> *Life changes*

Depressive feelings can also result from certain SUBSTANCES and MEDICATIONS. Even a sustained SUGAR- and CARB-HEAVY diet can cause you to feel depressed. HORMONES can also be a factor.

Don't discount the effects of WINTER months, either. Many people experience a slump in mood with the SHORTER DAYS, LONGER NIGHTS and reduced SUNLIGHT. In fact, S.A.D. (Seasonal Affective Disorder) is a recognised condition in some people during the winter season.

Rushing to see depression as an illness is
DISEMPOWERING. It can make you feel like a VICTIM.

There is much you can do to HEAL YOURSELF. Settling
for your LIMITATIONS keeps you from moving forward
and reclaiming your life.

Some things are in your POWER, some are NOT. Things
that ARE in your power are:

What you think

Who you choose to spend time with

How you react to situations

How you feel about yourself

What you do with your life

Things that are NOT in your power are:

Other people's behaviour

Other people's opinions of you

Other people's life choices

World events*

Forces of nature*

The weather*

The idea is to invest your energy only in those things
that you CAN control and MAKE PEACE with the rest.

---

*Although HUMANITY, as a whole, has some part to play in this.

WORKING DAY 8

- Could your depression be a result of your LIFESTYLE?

- Consult with a doctor to see if there are any EXACERBATING FACTORS causing you to feel depressed.

- If S.A.D. rings a bell, there are things you can do to offset the winter blues, such as remaining ACTIVE, going for WALKS in daylight, getting as much exposure to LIGHT as possible (even strong, artificial light can help) and avoiding STODGY FOOD.

- List the things that you think depression stops you from doing or achieving. Phrase them in the same way as the following example:

  'I want to enjoy life but I have depression.'

  Now relist the items, changing 'but' into 'and'. Notice how 'but' creates a STOP SIGN, while 'and' is just a SPEED BUMP.

In fact, go one step further and change the statement from 'I have depression' to 'I have a tendency to feel depressed'.

Now think of ways you can DRIVE OVER that speed bump.

- List the things that you are CAPABLE of doing if you stop ARGUING for your LIMITATIONS.

Aim for something of a higher value to ALIGN with and make that your TOUCHSTONE. For example, you might choose to align with 'love'. Ask yourself:

> 'How would I deal with this if I was loving towards myself, others and life?'
>
> 'How would I be thinking/acting/speaking if I was being loving?'

YOUR
MANTRA
FOR
DAY 8

'I am BIGGER than this.
I can move on, whenever I let go
of reasons NOT TO.'

DAY 9

Only
the
LONELY

You've CUT yourself OFF, haven't you?

You feel that no-one can UNDERSTAND, or that they wouldn't want to HANG OUT with you when you're like this.

Perhaps you feel that you just can't find the ENERGY to engage or that people are just TOO HARD to deal with.

Perhaps you have checked out because you've been HURT and it's SAFER not to risk intimacy again.

So, here you are – it's SIMPLER to disengage, isn't it? No HASSLES, no STRESS, no need to EXPLAIN YOURSELF.

All good – except for the fact that you're LONELY!

Maybe this is not a new feeling for you. You may feel depressed because you have always felt like an OUTSIDER. In other words, you may feel depressed BECAUSE you are lonely.

But OTHERS haven't isolated you – YOU have isolated YOURSELF, and it's time to take the first steps to engaging more with others and the world.

We ALL need the company of others, no matter how reclusive you have convinced yourself that you are. Being with others helps us to EXPAND, STEP OUT of OURSELVES and see life from different PERSPECTIVES. Being connected also boosts PHYSICAL HEALTH. In fact, human beings are HARD-WIRED to connect. That's why so much heartache arises from experiences of REJECTION or ABANDONMENT.

How DEEPLY you wish to connect is up to you. You don't have to commit to an intimacy you're not comfortable with! Even online connections are better than NONE.

However, it's important to be a little CHOOSY about who you hang out with. Did you know that being around POSITIVE people increases your capacity for happiness by 15 per cent per person? (The reverse is also true!) Stock up on seven happy people to spend time with and you may never LOOK BACK!

It is also important that you do this simply because it will FEEL GOOD to engage with others, not because you NEED them. Coming from NEED can push that which you desire away.

Stop seeing this as some kind of COMPETITION or TEST. Your assignment is simply to CONNECT, and the more you can ACCEPT people just as they ARE and ENJOY them – rather than worrying about fitting in – the more likely you are to be ACCEPTED.

Don't make it the BE ALL AND END ALL. Take it as it COMES. You'll have times when you CLICK and times when you DON'T – this happens to EVERYONE! Keep reaching out till you find the right mix for you.

It may feel SCARY at first, but things are only scary when they're UNFAMILIAR. Keep at it and, in time, you'll build your confidence.

WORKING DAY 9

- Today, start with some SMALL and SIMPLE interactions, such as a chat with a shopkeeper or a neighbour.

- Explore an INTEREST to share. www.meetup.com is one online organisation that brings together social and interest groups. There are literally THOUSANDS of outings and meetings you can join, and you need only attend when and how often it suits you. You might also look for interest groups and social activities in your area via the local library.

- Take YOURSELF out! Imagine you're on a 'date' with yourself. Go to a movie, a concert or a gallery. See it as a TREAT. SAVOUR the pleasure of being INDEPENDENT and free to do as you WISH.

- Get a PET or, if you can't have a pet, go to a dog park and hang out with some friendly fur-buddies. Usually they come with friendly OWNERS, too! You could also offer to walk your neighbour's dog if they're at work all day.

- VOLUNTEER. Not only will you be helping OTHERS, you'll also meet LIKE-MINDED people and you'll be taking your mind off YOUR troubles.

- Develop your own HANG OUT. Go to the same friendly café regularly. Take a book or read the paper. In time, you will develop a relationship with the STAFF and come to know other REGULARS.

YOUR
MANTRAS
FOR
DAY 9

*'Why should I fear being JUDGED
for making FRIENDS?'*

*'If I value MYSELF, I will be
valued by OTHERS.'*

DAY 10

Little old
ANGRY
ME

Depression was described by Sigmund Freud as *anger turned inward*.

This inner anger is really anger towards OTHERS that you have suppressed because:

> You were DEPENDENT on them
>
> They had CONTROL over you
>
> You feared that you would be ABANDONED if you showed your FEELINGS
>
> You feared being REJECTED if you weren't COMPLIANT or NICE

SELF-HATE can be described as *taking revenge on yourself for the faults of others*. In other words, we TURN on OURSELVES instead of others, and we do this because:

> Others may have seemed, or seem, too scary to confront
>
> Especially in childhood, we are afraid to see fault in those we rely on because we fear this puts our survival at risk, so we blame ourselves instead
>
> We desperately seek love and approval, and if let down, we assume it's because we're not lovable or worthy
>
> We buy into someone else's judgement and criticisms of us

The PROBLEM is that when you don't love yourself, you end up doing to YOURSELF the VERY THINGS you feared others would do to you! These things include:

Abandonment

Harsh judgement

Self-sabotage

Self-harm

Feeling lonely

When you become angry with yourself, you release an INNER BULLY who tells you that you're PATHETIC, UNWORTHY, HOPELESS, WEAK and/or downright BAD.

We tend to SUPPRESS anger because we FEAR it, but ANGER in itself is not necessarily a BAD thing. Anger is a NATURAL EMOTION that can MOTIVATE you, and help you to STAND UP for what you believe and to ASSERT yourself in a healthy way. It is not ANGER that is the issue, but how you HANDLE it.

Anger let loose without limitation can become AGGRESSION or even VIOLENCE. But anger turned INWARD without limitation becomes excessive SELF-CRITICISM and LOW SELF-ESTEEM and, in the end, DEPRESSION. None of these states is HEALTHY.

So, what to do with that SELF-DESTRUCTIVE anger?

> *Get it out! Express it in a non-violent and non-self-hating way (there are tips on the 'working' page).*

> *Forget trying to get someone ELSE to make amends! They may never apologise, be loving or even believe that they've done anything WRONG!*

> *Recognise the inner critic for what it is – a CRUEL BULLY who is pushing you into suffering.*

> *Get angry at the inner bully! Stand up to the attacks on your own behalf as a GOOD FRIEND would.*

Oh and, by the way, you can DISAGREE with your critics – that is, once you stop BELIEVING and INVESTING in the criticisms!

WORKING DAY 10

- Bash a PILLOW.

- YELL underwater.

- SCREAM in your car.

- BASH something inanimate.

- WRITE a letter.

- SPEAK it out.

- Imagine that the person who hurt you is sitting opposite you. Tell them how you FEEL. Get it off YOUR CHEST.

- What if you didn't BELIEVE those criticisms of you? Try not to buy into or invest in negative self-talk.

- What if you were simply NICER to yourself? Show yourself a little kindness and focus on some of your good qualities – we all have them!

- Take another look at the list mentioned on page 65. ACKNOWLEDGE how you might have subjected YOURSELF to what you feel OTHERS have subjected you to:

  Abandonment

  Harsh judgement

  Self-sabotage

  Self-harm

  Feeling lonely

YOUR MANTRA FOR DAY 10

'I now stand BY myself, FOR myself.'

DAY 11

Lessons
from
SIRI

Where you wind up emotionally has nothing to do with EXTERNAL circumstances and EVERYTHING to do with how you navigate your THOUGHTS ABOUT and RESPONSES TO external circumstances.

Though it may seem that the things that have happened to you CAUSE your feelings of despair, anger, hurt or self-loathing, they are really just OBSTACLES for you to steer past on your way to where you are really meant to be. So, it's important to set your DESTINATION, keep heading in that DIRECTION, and trust that you'll GET THERE.

The main reason people don't get to RECOVERY is that they keep making DETOURS, come to a dead stop at OBSTACLES, and often even turn RIGHT AROUND and head back to Misery Town if they think the journey is taking TOO LONG!

It's not what has happened to you that makes the difference – it's where you steer your thoughts ABOUT what's happened to you. Turn LEFT and losing your job is a DISASTER; turn RIGHT and it's now an opportunity to find something BETTER.

You cannot travel from one emotional state to another without an intervening thought TAKING you there. You cannot go from HAPPY to SAD, or from CALM to ANGRY, without thinking that there's something to be SAD or ANGRY about.

The key to turning around ANYTHING that disturbs you is to keep steering your THOUGHTS in the RIGHT DIRECTION, which means CHOOSING to adopt positive and empowering perspectives on your situation.

Most of us are SLOPPY about this and, unless we are on top of our thinking, it is easy to go from a few random negative thoughts to inner talk that sends you over the CLIFF!

Every thought acts as a kind of COMMAND. You set the 'destination' of your FEELINGS by what you THINK about, just like keying in a destination on your SATNAV.

If you can really get a grasp on the idea that you are the DRIVER of your thoughts and, as a result, your EXPERIENCE, then you must accept that you have the POWER to determine the OUTCOME.

Why are you letting your mind drive you into BAD NEIGHBOURHOODS, along rutted uncomfortable TRACKS or even over CLIFFS? Your mind is a TOOL that you can use any way you wish.

Who is in your DRIVER'S SEAT? Do you let your MIND take you wherever IT wants to go? Do you really think you have no SAY in the matter? You are not the HELPLESS VICTIM of your thoughts. YOU are the one in CHARGE of them. Do not think the mind is in control of you. It is YOUR mind. YOU get to decide which direction it is headed – TOWARDS or AWAY FROM your desired destination.

Of course when you first take back the steering wheel, it's going to feel STRANGE. Your mind has been on autopilot for so long, it will be used to going wherever IT wants.

But keep CALMLY and FIRMLY steering back onto the right road and it will have no other option but to COMPLY.

Think of the QUIET but PERSISTENT voice of your SATNAV. It may tell you that a certain street is in one direction but you don't TRUST it and keep driving. SIRI doesn't get FRUSTRATED or ANGRY, she simply tells you to turn around and TRY AGAIN. This is the same as your INNER GUIDANCE. It is that quiet voice telling you which way to TURN.

In time you'll learn to TRUST your INTUITION to keep you on track and stop you from making detours into DEAD ENDS or veering off into DITCHES.

WORKING DAY II

- Imagine that you have your own SIRI on board. You will know that it's SIRI when the voice is CALM, PATIENT and never gets UPSET. When your thoughts are heading in the right direction, you will feel CALM and CLEAR. Let your inner SIRI steer you through the day.

- Become a 'COULDA' – 'I could have talked myself into a dark place but I didn't.'

- When your thoughts stray (as they will), it doesn't mean that you're doing something WRONG – it simply means that you took a DETOUR down an UNHELPFUL path. Turn around and get back on track. Practise using feeling bad as your GUIDANCE SYSTEM, indicating to you when you've steered off course.

- Your mind is programmed to focus on what INTERESTS you the most! Notice what is grabbing most of your ATTENTION and what is occupying your THOUGHTS the most. Is it what you'd like to find MORE OF?

YOUR
MANTRAS
FOR
DAY II

*'My mind is SHAPED by
what I FOCUS upon.'*

*'My experience is what I CHOOSE
to give my attention to.'*

DAY 12

D.I.Y
brain
surgery

Did you know you can actually CHANGE the way your BRAIN works?

If you doubt this, think about the changes that have occurred since you became DEPRESSED.

You've managed to:

> *Develop insomnia*
>
> *Lose your appetite or eat more*
>
> *Feel guilty for no reason*
>
> *Feel irritable*
>
> *Stop enjoying life*
>
> *Have trouble interacting with others*
>
> *Feel that everything is hopeless*

While it can be argued that it's DEPRESSION causing these symptoms, blaming the depression is putting THE CART BEFORE THE HORSE.

If you do something OFTEN enough, such as thinking in a negative way over a sustained period of time, you are guaranteed to change the way your brain works.

The emphasis on thinking in a more positive way is not just WISHFUL THINKING. In attending to your thoughts, you are actually able to undo the damage that has been instilled through having a long-term pessimistic view.

The BOTTOM LINE is:

> *You cannot keep thinking in a DEPRESSED way –*
> *in a way that brings you DOWN – and expect to*
> *feel HAPPIER!*

Consider this: *There are no idle thoughts.*

The thoughts you have about the EVENTS, SITUATIONS
and PEOPLE in your life are really just OPINIONS about
what you are encountering. However, those OPINIONS
can make something feel like HEAVEN or HELL,
depending on what you're TELLING YOURSELF.

Every thought is CREATIVE.

Many of us aren't very good at thinking WELL, and
most of us let our thoughts ramble, undisciplined and
erratic, anywhere they like, which is how we get into
these emotional messes. Learning to CLEAN UP your
thinking is the single most HEALING thing you can do.

The most common errors in thinking are:

TOO QUICKLY DRAWING CONCLUSIONS WITHOUT
EVIDENCE

'I'm sure they're all angry with me.'

GENERALISATIONS

'Nothing good ever happens to me.'

PERSONALISATION

'She's not talking much. She must be unhappy with me.'

BULLYING THOUGHTS

'I'm an idiot!'

MAGNIFYING THE NEGATIVE/IGNORING THE POSITIVE

'The day was completely ruined.'

CATASTROPHISING

'I just know something terrible is going to happen.'

POLARISING

'I can see no good in this.'

MIND-READING

'I know you're thinking the worst of me.'

BLAMING

'It's not my fault! They did this to me!'

Each time you respond to events by thinking in a NEGATIVE, PESSIMISTIC or SELF-PUNISHING way, you are building a BRIDGE to the part of your brain that registers UNHAPPINESS. Do this often enough and that bridge becomes a FREEWAY that takes you DIRECTLY to that dark place by default, even with the most MINOR stimulus.

You find yourself seeing problems in the most innocuous situations and turning those perceived PROBLEMS into DISASTERS, and NORMAL LOSSES into TRAGEDIES.

Constantly REACTING to life in this way not only causes you to become overly SENSITISED, it also generates the STRESS CHEMICALS that cause you to feel depressed!

Something needs to CHANGE. You need to do a little BRAIN SURGERY to build a NEW BRIDGE, which will lead you to the FEEL-GOOD chemicals you need to bring you back into BALANCE.

The construction of the bridge requires you to step back before you REACT and CHOOSE to think in a more SUPPORTIVE way, so that a DIFFERENT, more feel-good part of your brain is activated. In other words, you need to learn to RESPOND calmly and practically to challenges, instead of blindly REACTING.

Do this often enough and not only do you start heading more AUTOMATICALLY via your new bridge to the better-feeling place in your brain, but you simultaneously start to feel the old bridge deteriorating through LACK OF USE!

You can actually CHANGE YOUR BRAIN! You're THAT POWERFUL!

It's not a QUICK FIX and it won't happen overnight, but you can start laying the FOUNDATIONS right now. Practise makes perfect.

(For a more in-depth explanation of this process, see my newly revised and expanded edition of *Taming the Black Dog*.)

WORKING DAY 12

- Today, be EXTRA CAREFUL with your thoughts. Monitor EVERY SINGLE thought so that you are AWARE of the main messages in your thinking. Don't JUDGE this process – just observe the relationship between what you're TELLING YOURSELF and how you FEEL.

- Divide a page into two columns. In the LEFT-HAND column, write down the thoughts you have noticed are the most DEPRESSING. Now, in the RIGHT-HAND column, write down what ELSE you could tell yourself that would be more UPLIFTING.

- Imagine that you are constructing a new bridge starting from today. What might be the first thing that you could change in your thinking to lay a fresh foundation?

YOUR MANTRA FOR DAY 12

*'I can burn old bridges when
I build NEW ones.'*

DAY 13

Does
it
HELP?

Beliefs are not FACTS. Often we hold on to outdated beliefs – usually about our limitations – without revisiting, exploring or refuting them, such as 'I'm no good at sport'. Where did you LEARN that? Is it still TRUE? Was it EVER true? And above all, does it HELP?

We unquestioningly adopt attitudes and ideas that may have been handed down for GENERATIONS and may never have been accurate or helpful in the first place!

You might still be abiding by the 'family religion' – the code of ethics and practices that were initiated within your family or culture 200 YEARS AGO!

The question is: are these beliefs HELPFUL to you? Or are they ideas that are actually doing you HARM?

In the movie, *Bridge of Spies*, Tom Hanks plays an agent during the Cold War who is assigned to return a Russian spy to his home country. During their time together, the two men form an unlikely bond. Eventually, the time comes for the Russian to be handed over. His fate is unclear – he may be welcomed back as a HERO or ASSASSINATED.

'Aren't you AFRAID?' the Hanks character asks his remarkably calm prisoner.

'Would it HELP?' is the man's reply.

As we have already explored, your THOUGHTS govern your FEELINGS, and, in particular, the beliefs that you have about something affect your EXPERIENCE of them.

Basically, if you BELIEVE something is TRUE, it will be true for YOU.

If you are constantly revisiting REGRETS, HURTS or GLOOMY PREDICTIONS, or WORRYING excessively, asking yourself whether or not this line of thinking is HELPFUL is a great tool to use from here on.

Feeling BAD can become a HABIT. Do you actually LOOK FOR things that MAKE and KEEP you miserable?

Why would we do this? We do it because there is an emotional PAYOFF.

These payoffs include:

> *Gaining SYMPATHY*
> *Being LOOKED AFTER or having people WORRY about you*
> *Not having to TRY*
> *JUSTIFYING staying STUCK*

And we CONTINUE doing it until there is no payoff except PAIN; until the habit no longer HELPS. That is when CHANGE can happen.

UNHELPFUL BELIEFS can include:

> *I'm too difficult to love*
> *I can't be loved because I'm too damaged*
> *Life is out to get me*
> *People always hurt me*
> *I never get anywhere in life*

Do these beliefs help you feel LESS DEPRESSED?
Do they HELP?

Time to let them GO then, eh?

WORKING DAY 13

- Make a list of the things you believe you are NOT GOOD at – for example, drawing, particular sports, etc. Now explore the following:

- Where did you LEARN that? Is this really TRUE or did you just stop TRYING because you BELIEVED it was true? Why did you come to think it WAS true?

- Write down some of the beliefs that you hold about depression (for example, that you are stuck with it). Do they HELP you to feel LESS DEPRESSED?

- Today, notice your conversations, both with others and internally with your self-talk. Are they HELPFUL or HARMFUL?

- Notice any thoughts about what could go wrong, such as 'I bet it won't work'. Say instead, 'I accept the challenge.'

YOUR MANTRA FOR DAY 13

'Is it TRUE? Does it HELP?'

DAY 14

It
don't
MEAN
a THING

Ceci n'est pas une chaise

A thing is just a THING, an experience is just an EXPERIENCE, a statement is just a BUNCH OF WORDS, a person is neither innately a FRIEND nor an ENEMY, and an event is neither PLEASANT nor UNPLEASANT – that is, until we place a MEANING onto these things.

It's not the thing, experience, statement, person or event that is the cause of your emotional distress – it is the MEANING that you give these that is doing you harm.

Someone will experience a room as uncomfortably HOT, while someone else thinks that it's COLD. Who is RIGHT about this?

A bride might be DEVASTATED that it is raining on her outdoor wedding, whereas a drought-affected farmer might welcome showers with CARTWHEELS of JOY.

In order to experience something in a certain way, you need to view it through a FILTER.

This filter is made up of your:

Conditioning
Past experiences
Expectations
Prejudices
Biases

Say there is a CHAIR in the corner of your room. In and of itself, it is just a CHAIR – in fact, it's not even a chair (people CALL it a 'chair') but an assembly of wood or metal and fabric. It is just a THING, with no particular MEANING beyond its basic FUNCTION.

But what if it was a PRECIOUS HEIRLOOM? What if it was the chair that your MOTHER sat in to nurse you? What if it was the first piece of furniture you BOUGHT for yourself? What if it was the only thing you SAVED from a house fire? What if you actually HATED that chair but your spouse refused to throw it out?

In any of these situations, you would have given the assembly of wood and fabric also known as a chair a MEANING, and now when you look at that chair, you FEEL a certain way about it.

We give meaning to EVERYTHING we encounter. We think that this means X and that means Y. And if X is a negative meaning, it will cause you to feel negative; and if Y is a positive meaning, it will invoke a positive response when you think about it. So the simple solution is to CHANGE THE MEANING!

Better still, REMOVE all meaning, and the feelings will disappear completely.

People who have overcome major challenges have simply changed the MEANING of whatever 'tragedy' or 'disaster' they have encountered into something that SUPPORTS them. The 'tragedy' or 'disaster' may now come to mean an 'awakening' or 'turning point' in their lives that motivated them to BETTER THEMSELVES or to help others who may have suffered in the same way. This changes the meaning of the tragedy into something that may actually be seen as CRUCIAL or even HELPFUL in the big picture.

The new meaning that they have given to their struggle is that it was a CATALYST for positive change.

Losing your job doesn't have to mean you are HOPELESS. The end of a relationship doesn't have to mean that you are UNLOVABLE. The loss of someone close doesn't have to mean that your life STOPS, too. Your brutal childhood doesn't have to mean that your adulthood is a MESS, too.

WORKING DAY 14

- How might you give your past challenges a NEW MEANING?

- Step back from the events of the day and see them from a NEUTRAL position. Simply witness and observe them without attaching any particular MEANING to them.

YOUR MANTRAS FOR DAY 14

'I get to DECIDE what this MEANS.'

'Shall I make the meaning SAD or GLAD?'

DAY 15

Dare
to be
GRATEFUL

You have NOTHING, right? Everything is LOST, isn't it?

Well, it can certainly FEEL that way when you have depression.

Now, I'm going to sound like a PREACHY PARENT here, but hey ...

Honestly, are you really THAT badly off?

Some people have BOMBS raining down on their heads, some people are STARVING. Really THINK about that.

But I get it – those concepts can all seem very far away and abstract from where you are. You're looking at your life and it seems DESOLATE and EMPTY.

As challenging as it may seem in your current situation, indulging in a bit of GRATITUDE can actually do wonders for your OWN wellbeing.

How? You start to see what's WORKING instead of what's NOT working. You start to realise how much is actually going FOR you instead of against. You start to see and APPRECIATE the nice things all around you that your depressed state has blinded you to. The more you focus on the good things you have, the more good things you ATTRACT.

Really, come to think of it, how dare you NOT be grateful?

Most likely, you have FOOD in your belly, a WARM BED, a ROOF over your head, MONEY to buy this book (or a library that will lend it to you for free).

No matter how little you feel you have, you have something precious – your BODY and your MIND.

Imagine that you are being asked to do a final inventory of the good things you have had in your life. You might be tempted to say that you had nothing good. In which case, you would have left out FLOWERS, BIRDS, TREES, WIND, SUN, RAIN, THE OCEANS, ANIMALS, FOOD, RAINBOWS, COLOURS, LIGHT – in fact, the ENTIRE PLANET, which is at your disposal.

Are you taking these precious things for GRANTED? Are you actually even TRASHING these things? You are at a BANQUET! Why are you choosing CRUMBS?

If you don't APPRECIATE things – if you don't cherish them, nurture them and look after them – they can slip away or shrivel from neglect, in which case, you may perceive that you have LOST these things, where in truth, you just needed to VALUE them more. And most importantly, you need to value YOURSELF.

Gratitude is one of the most POWERFUL tools you can use to turn around the way you feel. While this is an exercise just for today, you will see the best results if you make this a DAILY PRACTICE.

Gratitude releases FEEL-GOOD HORMONES, such as *dopamine, serotonin* and *oxytocin,* and helps build deeper positive connections with YOURSELF, OTHERS and LIFE.

And ... gratitude works especially well when you can feel grateful even when you can't see any reason to be!

Although you may feel like the UNLUCKIEST person on the planet when you start on this work, if you want to see some quick-fire improvements, it's time to get some GRATITUDE!

Do not underestimate the power of gratitude.

In fact, gratitude can work like MAGIC. The more you APPRECIATE, the more you will see good things showing up in your own life. LIKE ATTRACTS LIKE.

WORKING DAY 15

- Being GRATEFUL is a CHOICE. CHOOSE to be grateful today.

- Do something nice for others as often as possible today. Here are some ideas:

  Write to someone expressing your appreciation

  Thank service people you encounter

  Compliment someone

  Give way to a driver

- Post an expression of APPRECIATION for something on social media (e.g., 'Beautiful sunrise today').

- Ban all WHINGEING or COMPLAINING today!

- Start a GRATITUDE JOURNAL. Begin by listing:

  Three things to thank yourself for doing well today

  Three things that went well today

  Three things in your life that are good

  Three people who have been kind to you or have supported you

And take it from there. See how many more items you can add to the list each day.

- Recall a DIFFICULT time from the past. Obviously you got through it. Be GRATEFUL for the way you OVERCAME this. You can do it AGAIN!

- Notice the good things in life and AMPLIFY your APPRECIATION of them – such as the TASTE of food; the SMELL of NATURE; the LOVE that your friends, family, partner or pet offers you.

- Finally, look in the mirror. Tell that person that s/he is of VALUE.

YOUR MANTRA FOR DAY 15

'There ARE things in my life to be grateful for.'

DAY 16

Be careful what you ASK for

You may not have been aware of this before but, more often than you realise, you have been lining up with what you've ASKED FOR!

That job that you lost – didn't you COMPLAIN about it?

That relationship that ended – was it really WORKING?

Those friends who 'abandoned' you – were they TRUE friends?

Those people who treated you BADLY – were you setting clear LIMITS and BOUNDARIES?

And those who DISRESPECTED you – did you INVITE respect? Did you respect YOURSELF?

Perhaps these things that you THOUGHT were 'taken away' from you were not actually RIGHT for you, and now that they have gone, there is room for something ELSE and something BETTER to come along!

Depression very much centres on what we feel we have LOST, rather than what we HAVE.

And in EXPECTING the worst, we tend to INVITE IN the worst.

If you don't want to keep attracting the same old crap, you need to start ASKING FOR and EXPECTING something BETTER.

If you keep harping on about how things will never work out or that your life is hopeless, you will actually REPEL anything good from entering your life, because thinking in this way means that good things are not a MATCH with where you're at.

You need to put yourself in the same ZONE as the good things you want to experience.

So how do you do that if you are feeling MISERABLE?

You can start to make small shifts in your mood by simply going more NEUTRAL. Instead of allowing a NEGATIVE running commentary to dominate your thinking, use the practices of Day 14 and suspend making ANY opinion on things, GOOD or BAD.

MANIFESTING what you want is possible, but it involves a few steps:

1. Believing that you can have good things

   This might feel like a STRETCH, but you need to believe that something is POSSIBLE for you to experience evidence of it in your life.

2. Forming a clear vision of what you want

   However, you don't need to have the specifics of the THING in mind (though this can help) as much as the FEELING of having it. It's the FEELING that we're aiming for.

3. Expecting it to happen

   No IFS or BUTS. You need to have the same quiet,
   confident FAITH that what you want will show up, as
   you do that the sun will rise tomorrow. You don't lie
   awake fretting about whether the sun will do that
   (or maybe you do!); you just KNOW that it will.

4. Forgetting about it

   Once you have it locked in, you don't need to
   keep checking the mailbox or opening the door to
   see if it's there. KNOW that it WILL be there.

5. The form may be different from your
   expectations

   The aim is the FEELING, remember? So you
   thought that you would get that feeling from
   having a red sports car, but you actually got that
   same feeling from someone being KIND to you.

You can TRANSFORM your world when you get the
hang of this. Today is a chance to EXPERIMENT.

Pay more attention to what's WORKING, what you
ENJOY and what feels GOOD, and AMPLIFY these things
by reporting aloud the positive qualities you observe.
For example, 'This is such a DELICIOUS salad! The
vegetables are really FRESH. I love the vivid colour
of the tomatoes.'

This is especially effective if you can SHARE your comments with others, as you then see reflected the impact of more positive statements and how they make you and others feel BETTER.

WORKING DAY 16

- Start small and build up by putting it out there that you'd like a small, pleasant SURPRISE to show up today. It doesn't matter WHAT it is, just ask for the FEELING of having something NICE appear.

- Apply the principles to:

    Securing a parking spot
    Having the traffic lights stay green
    Finding a lost object

- Observe how you ATTRACT things into your life. Have a little FUN with this by choosing a symbol to watch out for today – perhaps a BLUE CIRCLE or a RED BIRD or a YELLOW CAR. Notice how often it shows up.

- Reflect on the things you felt had been 'taken away' from you. What happened next? Was it for the BETTER?

- How might you make a CURRENT challenge turn out to be 'for the better'?

YOUR
MANTRA
FOR
DAY 16

*'Today I am exploring being
the CREATOR in my
world instead of a
VICTIM of circumstances.'*

DAY 17

I'm
OUTTA
here

Today, we need to talk about the ELEPHANT in the room – SUICIDE.

For many of you, this may never be a SERIOUS option; for others, you may at times FANTASISE along these lines; and for the rest, you have either seriously contemplated the notion of SUICIDE or may actually have come to the BRINK of carrying it through.

There are many reasons why suicide may seem to be some sort of SOLUTION. These may include:

> *Showing others how much they have hurt you*
>
> *Finding respite and rest from the torment you are experiencing*
>
> *An attempt to convey your struggle when you feel unheard*
>
> *An idea that you will find something 'better' on the other side*
>
> *Feeling that you are so loathsome that you do not deserve to live*
>
> *Feeling that things can never improve*
>
> *An idea that those closest to you will be better off without you*

While these feelings might lead you to the idea that suicide is some form of SOLUTION, it's NOT.

Like it or not, you are here for the LONG HAUL.

However, if the option of escaping your current struggles by taking your own life is removed, you may be left wondering how you will COPE.

And the answer is, you WILL cope because that is what you need to do now. You need to find another, more healthy solution.

Acknowledge that you are not really THINKING STRAIGHT, are you? Are you really in the best position to make such a MONUMENTAL, IRREVERSIBLE decision?

No, you're NOT. When you are depressed you are not YOURSELF. You are not ACCURATELY gauging the situation. You are not seeing things STRAIGHT.

Dead is DEAD. No half measures. There's no such thing as 'Whoops, I've changed my mind' dead.

And what if you BOTCH it? MORE suffering – even GREATER suffering – and it's not only YOU who will suffer.

Suicide is NOT FOR YOU. FORGET it. It's a BAD idea all round.

WORKING DAY 17

- Even if suicide has not been a serious option for you, it's time to make ABSOLUTELY SURE that it never is.

Today, I want you to do a little ritual. Close your eyes and imagine that you are standing in the middle of a courtyard. You are surrounded by high walls, which you can't see over at this point. On the LEFT is a door marked SUICIDE. On the RIGHT is a door marked STAY STUCK. Behind you is a door that is marked THE PAST, and ahead of you is a door marked THE FUTURE. At your feet are some implements, including a heavy chain, planks of wood and nails, a drill and screws, and padlocks with keys.

In your mind, go over to the SUICIDE door. I want you to SECURE that door so that it can never be opened. Use ALL of the implements at your disposal. Make sure it is IMPENETRABLE. Now say to yourself, 'I will never open this door' and throw the key over the wall.

Do the same for THE PAST. Say, 'The past is done. If I open this door it will only be to see how far I've come.' Now place a chain through the door handle and padlock the door. You may keep the key or you might throw it away completely. The choice is yours. But as you have the key, you must use it WISELY.

Next, you need to make a CHOICE. You can remain where you are. If you do make this choice, you need to see what this involves. Open the STAY STUCK door, where NOTHING changes. Have a good look around this enclosed space. How long do you intend to stay here, looking at this? Will you lock the door and throw away the key?

You may choose the last door – THE FUTURE. You will not know what is behind it and there are no GUARANTEES. You will need to take what you get. But it is an EXIT from any situation you find yourself in. Do you choose it?

- Write down the first steps you will take to COPE, because now you must cope. They may be SMALL steps but they are the steps you need to take now.

- And if you're still considering SUICIDE, CALL SOMEONE. NOW! Better still, LINE UP someone in ADVANCE to talk to. Ask them if it's okay to call them if you need to.

- And here's another thing – wait until MORNING before you make any BIG DECISIONS. And if it's WINTER, wait until SPRING! (See the item on S.A.D. on page 49.) In fact, just WAIT. Think and think again.

YOUR
MANTRAS
FOR
DAY 17

*'I CAN cope. I WILL cope.
I am ALREADY coping.'*

*'All things PASS.
Even this pain will pass.'*

DAY 18

The
WORLD'S
gone
to
SHIT

'Yeah, yeah,' you say. 'So I STICK AROUND – but what for? The world is an UGLY place, full of CRUELTY and MEANNESS, not to mention the MESS the environment's in! It's hard to LOOK FORWARD to anything with all that bad shit going on.'

I hear you – it can certainly FEEL that way!

The world has always been MESSY, and it will never be PERFECT. Humans will ALWAYS encounter experiences in life that CONTRAST with what we would prefer but it is through these challenges that we EXPAND.

Without CHALLENGES and CONTRASTS, there would be no ADVANCEMENTS, NEW SOLUTIONS or BREAKTHROUGHS.

It's easy to invest in and foster an idea that the world has gone to the dogs but that's because we're more EXPOSED to world events than ever before and the media tends to practise SENSATIONALISM. BAD NEWS is always more INTERESTING and draws more attention!

But for every BAD NEWS story, there is another story of GENEROSITY, KINDNESS and SELFLESSNESS.

While INJUSTICES and INHUMAN ACTS do occur, many that have been swept under the carpet for decades have now been brought to light and have led to NECESSARY CHANGES.

Notice how this works. Someone messes up BIG TIME. This may appear to be a TRAGEDY of mammoth proportions at the time – there may be loss of life, severe damage to the environment or even acts of cruelty.

When we look at this in isolation, we are AGHAST. How can this possibly happen?

But look what can happen in response. If the deed is dastardly enough, there may follow PROTESTS, there may be INQUIRIES, OUTRAGE, DEMONSTRATIONS and even RECRIMINATIONS. The issue becomes front-page news. People DEMAND improvements and changes. They JOIN TOGETHER to support and bring about these changes in ways they have never done before. Then, lo and behold, a new LAW is created or a new THERAPY or a new SOLUTION, and when that is done, the world moves on to the NEXT THING.

This process will NEVER stop. As a SPECIES, we are continually EVOLVING and EXPANDING, and in order to do so, we are faced with MORE and BIGGER challenges. As humans, we must ACCEPT this and ADAPT.

The thing to remember is that we are ALL IN THIS TOGETHER.

On an INDIVIDUAL level, life may seem cruel; but in the big picture, it helps to take life less PERSONALLY and see it more GLOBALLY. This kind of thinking does require a more expanded perspective than you may have been used to but it does change the way things appear.

Unfortunately, the media and social media contribute greatly to the idea that the world is full of DANGER and VIOLENCE, but this version of the human story is strongly shaped by the influence of money in media and politics. FEAR SELLS.

In other words, by and large, we have been TAUGHT to be on the lookout for what is WRONG, but this is not the entire picture, nor is it the essential TRUTH.

The TRUTH is that the world is as it has ALWAYS been – a combination of BAD and GOOD, WRONG and RIGHT, HATRED and LOVE, UGLINESS and BEAUTY, and every human being has some INFLUENCE on this, through their own INPUT.

WORKING DAY 18

- Think about the wonderful INNOVATIONS that have resulted from what appeared at the time to be tragedies. For example, the first moon landing was made possible only after learning from earlier unsuccessful and tragic attempts, and vaccines were developed to protect against illnesses that once killed millions.

- Are we really WORSE off? Take a look through history and you will find TORTURE, DISEASE, POLLUTION, CRUELTY, CORRUPTION and POVERTY. Nothing new there.

- Search the internet for five examples of the GOOD in the world – for example, recycling innovations, animal rescue, health advancements or social improvements. You'll find them!

- Think of how the media needs to SENSATIONALISE. The news you read is selected for its IMPACT. The guy helping the kitten from the tree is not going to be front-page news. You may never hear about numerous acts of kindness but that doesn't mean they don't happen.

- How might YOU contribute to a BETTER world?

YOUR MANTRAS FOR DAY 18

'If I seek what is GOOD in the world,
I will find it, just as I can seek
what is BAD and find that.'

'I am an EQUAL contributor
to the reality I see.'

DAY 19

Host a
PITY
PARTY...

Today, instead of thinking, 'I shouldn't feel this way', allow yourself to give FULL REIN to your feelings.

You have a RIGHT to your feelings. You may have had things happen that have had a deep impact on you and possibly for some time.

When we bottle up emotions, they tend to IMPLODE. They become CONGESTED and INFLAMED, and it takes very little to set you off because of the stockpile of emotions that you are carrying around that have not been fully RELEASED and EXPRESSED.

However, there is a big difference between letting your emotions EXPLODE and actually RELEASING them in a HEALTHY way.

Pay particular attention to emotional responses such as ANGRY OUTBURSTS or EXCESSIVE CRYING.

The difference between RELEASE and INDULGENCE is that you will feel LIGHTER if you have released but more UPSET if you have indulged.

The best way to release emotions is to picture them as something LEAVING you. One of your exercises for today will help clarify this process.

Give yourself permission to GRIEVE, WAIL, RAIL AGAINST, RAGE, WEEP, SULK or whatever it takes to undertake an emotional DETOX.

If you're doing this properly, eventually one of two things is likely to happen:

(a) You are now UTTERLY SICK of feeling miserable (like when you've overindulged in chocolate mud cake), or

(b) You don't feel like CONTINUING with this day's exercises after a while.

Do them anyway – just prove to yourself that you really ARE willing to let this misery go and that you have wallowed in this long enough and are ready to move on.

WORKING DAY 19

- Close your eyes and imagine the EMOTIONAL LOAD you are carrying. How do you SEE this? What is its SHAPE? TEXTURE? COLOUR? SIZE? WHERE ARE YOU CARRYING IT? Try DRAWING it.

  Now, taking DEEP BREATHS, picture RELEASING the load in the appropriate way. For example, if it is a heavy OBJECT, how might you DISPOSE of it? Perhaps it takes the form of a DARK CLOUD – see that lifting off and away.

  Put aside some ME time today to set the stage for a right old PITY PARTY and – here's the thing –you are to totally INDULGE in doing this!

- Collect the following ammunition:

  Journal (the outpouring kind)

  Old photos

  Old love letters

  Music/movies that makes you sad

  Food you shouldn't eat

  A MODERATE amount of alcohol (I said MODERATE!)

  Tissues, a stuffed toy and a blanket

  Notebook and pen

- Approach this exercise GUILT-FREE. You are giving yourself PERMISSION to feel crap, instead of thinking you SHOULDN'T feel this way!

- Write down an exhaustive list of EVERYTHING that's WRONG in your world. Do not leave out ANYTHING!

- GRIEVE, RANT, WAIL – whatever! Go for it! The more TEARS the better! Tears are a healthy and natural way to RELEASE emotion.

- Keep going till you're DONE. Ideally, you'll feel TIRED, PURGED and totally OVER feeling SORRY FOR YOURSELF!

- Remember – EVERYONE feels this way at times, but this is about YOU releasing in a HEALTHY way!

- Copy the way CHILDREN release their emotions – FURIOUS with you one minute, then climbing onto your lap the next. Once it's OUT, it's DONE!

- Remember that you have just performed a CLEAN-OUT! Don't fill up the cupboards again!

YOUR MANTRA FOR DAY 19

'I have now made room for NEW and BETTER feelings.'

DAY 20

For
the
LAST
TIME

Depression and SELF-PITY go hand in hand. In fact, you can't have depression WITHOUT feeling sorry for yourself.

And while you and just about anyone might agree that you have PLENTY to feel sorry for yourself about, you need to drop SELF-PITY if you want to get WELL.

Self-pity is a STICKY TRAP. While there may be perfectly valid reasons to feel HARD DONE BY, this day is about 'stepping up' and embracing challenges instead of being sucked into the quicksand of self-pity.

Think about the opening statement here. IF YOU DROP SELF-PITY YOU ALSO DROP THE DEPRESSION.

Be honest, now – if you were not LAMENTING your lot you would have nothing to feel DEPRESSED about, would you?

This is a big one and you'll need to really work it by OWNING it and choosing to no longer INDULGE it.

However, do NOT beat yourself up when you get into self-pity. We all do it – it's just that you've made it your central focus and it has become a HABIT. Feeling BAD can develop into a HABIT – a habit that has got you into this place along with self-pity. Recognise when it's taking over and making you a VICTIM.

Facing down self-pity can be TOUGH but LIBERATING.

The temptation to find 'sickly comfort' from self-pity is persuasive but it is a poisonous trap.

Make ROOM for it as being part of depression. ROLL around in it for a while – if you must – then DON'T. It's a DECISION.

You may need to make that decision many times but MAKE IT. The more you catch yourself getting caught up in self-pity and make this choice, the more EMPOWERED you will feel and the more likely you will be to take POSITIVE ACTION.

WORKING DAY 20

- Think of all the things that you have been feeling DEPRESSED about. Write them down. Now rephrase them without SELF-PITY. How do they look to you now?

- Think of the things about which you feel sorry for yourself. Now apply the 3 Ps (a process developed by psychologist Martin Seligman):

PERSONALISATION
Have you REALLY been SINGLED OUT for PUNISHMENT? Could you really CONTROL all elements of what has happened?

PERVASIVENESS
Is the loss of ONE THING really the loss of EVERYTHING?

PERMANENCE
Does this really need to last FOREVER?

- The next time things don't go to PLAN, watch out for self-pitying statements (and attitudes) like: 'Things never go right for me! I have to do everything myself! No-one cares about my struggles', etc.

YOUR
MANTRA
FOR
DAY 20

'Self-pity does NOTHING to HELP what's wrong, other than to KEEP IT wrong.'

DAY 21

Hunting
down
HAPPINESS

So-called 'happiness experts' tell us that the secret to happiness is to 'remove negative thoughts'. You might actually think that is what I am asking of you; but, in fact, I've only asked you to seek out HELPFUL thoughts. You see, there's a TRAP to this – the minute you try NOT to do something, the MORE you do it!

Try this: don't think about a PINK GIRAFFE. I'll bet that all you're thinking about now is a pink giraffe!

So, if you can't actually REMOVE negative thoughts from your mind, how do you get past depression and start feeling HAPPIER?

Well, instead of trying to get RID of negative thoughts, the idea is to see things from a BROADER PERSPECTIVE.

For a start, as we've already explored, a THOUGHT is just a THOUGHT – just because you think it, doesn't make it GOSPEL. But, so far, that's how your thinking has gone, hasn't it? You THINK it's BAD, so it MUST be.

Hopefully, by now, you're starting to question the VALIDITY of this. If not, consider all the FEARS, DOUBTS and DIRE PREDICTIONS that have been your default position until now. How many of them were ACCURATE?

Instead of trying to ELIMINATE every negative thought (which will drive you even DEEPER into despair), the art is in seeing the thought from a DIFFERENT ANGLE, which means really considering whether the thought is actually VALID, whether it is a FACT or an ASSUMPTION, and whether it actually serves any useful PURPOSE.

Consider how many THOUGHTS you had yesterday. HUNDREDS, THOUSANDS, even. Where are they NOW? They are GONE. So much for the importance you placed on those fleeting ideas! But if we add them up, repeated in a certain way day after day, year after year, there is a lasting effect – in this case, you feel DEPRESSED.

So, let's examine how happy (or happier) people view things. Being happy does not make you IMMUNE from challenges, but what does happen is that the challenges have less IMPACT because they are seen from a more OPTIMISTIC PERSPECTIVE. So, a happier person might say: 'Okay, what can I DO about this?' Or: 'I'll give it a go at least. If that doesn't work, I'll look at something else.' Or: 'Does it really matter all that much if I mess it up?'

This day's work, therefore, is titled 'Hunting Down Happiness'. We think that happiness is the ULTIMATE GOAL, don't we? But the endless pursuit of happiness (with the accompanying idea that NOT being happy is somehow WRONG) is just as FUTILE as trying to totally avoid any negativity.

Happiness COMES and GOES, usually from unexpected sources. Trying to be happy all the time can also drive you crazy. So, again, what to do?

Aim for CONTENTMENT. Aim to be okay with whatever comes along. Aim to MAKE PEACE with life's ever-changing landscape. Aim to ACCEPT more the things that you have not accepted. And finally, seek out the things that DO give you pleasure. They may not actually be BIG things; instead, they could be small moments of CALM and CONTENTMENT that you have not noticed with your dark filter in place.

A great way to boost your OWN happiness quota is to boost SOMEONE ELSE'S! Being GENEROUS to another is actually a WIN-WIN result because BOTH parties feel uplifted! Depression can tend to lead you to be very SELF-FOCUSED. By actively GIVING to others, you not only do GOOD but you also extend beyond yourself and your previous feelings of LIMITATION and HELPLESSNESS.

WORKING DAY 21

- Today, notice any little fleeting moments of CALM, CONTENTMENT or even HAPPINESS that come to you, and jot down what you were doing at the time. You may be surprised to find that it's actually the SMALL, EVERYDAY things that bring joy, rather than big events.

- Think of one aspect of your life that currently causes you to feel OFF BALANCE but is easily FIXED. Do something about this one item.

- Do at least one of these things today:

  Call or meet up with a friend for
  a pleasant chat

  Exercise

  Work on a hobby or interest

  Take time out for the pleasure of it

  Walk in the sunshine

  Go to a concert, play or movie

- If you have too much unfocused time, RESEARCH and SIGN UP FOR a new passion. This may include:

    A good cause

    Volunteering

    Learning a new skill

    Writing or art

    Joining a club

    Enrolling in a course

- Be GENEROUS by:

    Making a donation

    Doing a favour for someone

    Indulging in a random act of kindness

    Visiting someone lonely

    Making positive comments on social media

YOUR
MANTRAS
FOR
DAY 21

'Happiness is FLEETING.'

'Being CONTENTED is a CHOICE.'

DAY 22

The BENEFITS of the BLUES

OK...onto the NEXT THING

RETRENCHMENT

There's nothing GOOD about depression, is there?

It's the WORST thing that could have happened to you, isn't it?

Or IS it?

Imagine if you had a MAGIC BUTTON that would immediately erase any feelings of SADNESS or DEPRESSION the moment they arose.

Sounds GREAT, right? Or DOES it?

Now try to picture your life without ANY of those feelings. Wouldn't it feel SHALLOW and ONE-DIMENSIONAL after a while?

Personally, the conventional idea of heaven as a perfect paradise where the sun SHINES every day, where people are always KIND and OBLIGING, where one is always in a state of BLISS and where every attempt is SUCCESSFUL would have me screaming with boredom after just a few days!

What would there be to feel EXCITED or PASSIONATE about if there were no feelings of YEARNING and LONGING to motivate you to seek out something MORE?

What if there was never anyone to CHAFE against to help you more clearly DEFINE and REFINE your character, embrace a different POINT OF VIEW and RESOLVE DIFFERENCES?

Without CHALLENGES, you would not EXPAND, because if you were 'Pollyanna' happy every minute of the day, there would be no reason to CHANGE or GROW.

Spending your life dodging painful emotions means that you deprive yourself of the DEPTH and CHARACTER-BUILDING that emotions – such as disappointment, heartbreak and self-doubt – can generate.

There can actually be BENEFITS in experiencing so-called 'negative' emotions, but only if you are willing to:

> *LEARN from them*
>
> *RISK new experiences (e.g., there is always a risk of sadness when you fall in love with someone)*
>
> *See the VALUE in these emotions motivating CHANGE, rather than STALLING change*

Interestingly, research has shown that people who see VALUE in their negative emotions are less BOTHERED by them than those who see negative emotions as something HARMFUL and to be AVOIDED.

WORKING DAY 22

- How might you USE your experience of depression to add MEANING to your life (and the lives of OTHERS)?

- Reflect on how so-called 'negative' feelings have motivated you to make necessary CHANGES in your life.

- Spend HALF of today being MISERABLE. Do not let ANYTHING cheer you up! Now spend the other half of the day being CHEERFUL. Do NOT let ANYTHING bring you down! Notice how it is virtually impossible to completely sustain either emotional state indefinitely.

- Today, focus on appreciating the CONTRASTS in your life and how each is VALID.

YOUR MANTRA FOR DAY 22

'Life is an eternal seesaw.
I am MEANT to go up and down –
but not stay STUCK on either end!'

DAY 23

MOVE ALONG –
nothing
to see here

(or set your
ELEPHANT free)

Holding on to the PAST is like trying to walk with an ELEPHANT on your back (and yes, it's a relative of the elephant from DAY 17).

It's very, very hard to go ANYWHERE with an elephant on your back!

Elephants are HEAVY, CUMBERSOME, NOISY and only helpful when you're the one doing the RIDING, not the other way around!

Letting go of the past is a DECISION to no longer let it WEIGH YOU DOWN.

When you hold on to the PAST, you let it DEFINE you and, too often, people use it as a JUSTIFICATION for their limitations:

> 'I can't be HAPPY because of what happened to me.'
>
> 'I can't find FULFILMENT today because I lost something back then.'
>
> 'I can't do this NEW THING / ACHIEVE A GOAL / LEARN THIS because I was CRITICISED or made FUN of when I tried before.'
>
> 'I was HURT the last time I trusted someone, therefore, NO-ONE is TRUSTWORTHY.'
>
> 'I did a HORRIBLE THING once, and that means I'm still a BAD person.'

'My life is FOREVER RUINED because of what was done to me.'

'I can never love ANYONE again after my love has gone.'

'I will never FORGIVE.'

Holding on to the PAST does NOTHING to improve what happened. It doesn't BRING PEOPLE BACK or make them say SORRY or even FEEL REGRET!

All it does is CHAIN you to that ELEPHANT. Nothing ELSE is achieved. Nothing is FIXED. Nothing is HEALED. Nothing is CHANGED for the better.

LOSING YOURSELF doesn't make 'them' sorry. Really, they couldn't CARE LESS! They may not even think they've done anything WRONG!

Once, those people who may have hurt you seemed to be BIGGER than you in some way, but that is no longer the case if you choose to EXPAND yourself.

The issue is not what happened THEN but what you DO NOW about what was done, instead of TORTURING yourself by HOLDING ON to it.

Whatever happened then is no longer in your CONTROL to change. It is important that you let go of the things over which you don't actually have any control – such as what other people do, or did.

The art in moving on is in becoming BIG enough yourself to not be threatened by others' SMALLNESS. To be able to look back and know that they taught you how NOT to be, and that you have become better than the example they showed you. The best REVENGE is to be happy.

And – here's an IMPORTANT point – your MIND shouldn't have to handle more than 24 HOURS at a time! Crowd it with any more than that and it becomes OVERWHELMED. This is why staying in the PRESENT is so important.

You know what? Your ELEPHANT would be just as happy to be free of YOU as you would be relieved to be free of HIM! It's time to FREE your ELEPHANT!

WORKING DAY 23

- Imagine your life is a PLAY and all the people in your life are CHARACTERS, each with a given role. There will be HEROES, VILLAINS, CAMEO PARTS, LEADING ROLES and EXTRAS. Write down the CAST of your PLAY and describe the CHARACTER of each member, including your OWN.

- What part do those in your PAST play in your CURRENT life? How might you change the SCRIPT to IMPROVE the relationship or DILUTE its impact?

- Try to LOCATE the PAST. Where does it actually EXIST? Realise that it cannot exist beyond your thoughts.

- TRY MEDITATION. Fifteen minutes daily is all it takes to make a BIG difference to your wellbeing over time. Simply close your eyes and bring your mind to the PRESENT every time it wanders off, by bringing your attention to your BREATH.

- TRY MINDFULNESS. Bring your FULL attention to THIS MOMENT. Notice fully what you are FEELING, HEARING, SEEING, SMELLING, TASTING and TOUCHING till all else falls away.

YOUR
MANTRA
FOR
DAY 23

'The PAST is GONE.
It does not EXIST beyond my THOUGHTS.'

DAY 24

Forgive
EVERYBODY –
especially
YOURSELF

The only sure way to lighten the load is to let everybody off the hook – especially YOURSELF.

This can seem like a MAJOR TASK if you feel you have been badly hurt, but there are ways of seeing things that make way for FORGIVENESS.

To hold resentment is to enslave YOURSELF. The more time you spend feeling resentful, the more you become tangled in the anger that arises from it, and you end up in emotional, psychological and spiritual bondage to the one you feel resentment TOWARDS. In the end, the one holding the resentment suffers most, and that is YOU.

Forgiveness is often confused with CONDONING bad behaviour, but forgiveness involves seeing the HUMAN behind the behaviour and having COMPASSION for someone's shortfalls.

This does not mean that the perpetrator is not ACCOUNTABLE for their acts; instead, it means that THEIR acts no longer have power over YOUR wellbeing.

In other words, you SET LOOSE the perpetrator to deal with the consequences of their actions according to their own conscience. It no longer has anything to do with you.

We often think that staying angry with someone is the only way to VALIDATE our own hurt and suffering, but hanging on does nothing to change what has happened, and only keeps you STUCK in a toxic emotional relationship with the person who has hurt you.

Stepping up to forgiveness means embracing a certain level of evolved consciousness. It means being BIGGER than another's smallness, LEARNING from the experience, ACCEPTING your own part in the dynamic (such as STICKING AROUND when you would have been best OUT OF THERE) and being willing to see the human flaws in ALL people.

There are ways to open up to this kind of thinking by contemplating the following:

> *People do what they do for their own reasons. These reasons may not be valid for you but are to the person who is acting on them.*
>
> *People do what they do because it fits their own 'story' of how they think things are.*
>
> *People do what they do only because they think doing it will make them feel better or will be helpful to them in some way.*
>
> *At the heart of even the most heinous act is someone in pain.*

*Until they are evolved, people are essentially
small children walking around in adult bodies.*

*A person who is evolved does not harm others.
A person who is afraid or threatened does.*

People teach you about yourself.

We teach people how to treat us.

Humans, on the whole, are still very much in SURVIVAL MODE and, as such, we often feel THREATENED or in COMPETITION with one another. Most of the time we are locked into POWER PLAYS because we feel we don't HAVE enough or that we ourselves are NOT ENOUGH.

This causes us to act in less than ideal ways – we TAKE what we can because we fear LOSING (or never having), or we GIVE AWAY our power to someone else because we fear NOT BEING LOVED.

In the end, there is only one thing behind 'bad' behaviour – FEAR. How might this affect the way you feel about someone else's behaviour now?

Forgiving YOURSELF for the same humanness is also VITAL. It's time to forgive EVERYBODY – including YOU!

In fact, you can learn much about YOURSELF from the way that people RESPOND to you. For example, if someone treats you DISRESPECTFULLY, what aspect of your OWN behaviour might you need to develop to prevent this happening again? Perhaps you might need to ASSERT yourself more or make BETTER CHOICES about who you associate with.

Seeing others as your MIRROR and making the necessary IMPROVEMENTS can transform them from ADVERSARIES to TEACHERS.

WORKING DAY 24

- Divide a page into TWO COLUMNS. In the left-hand column, write down the things that you have done that you are not proud of. Now on the right-hand side, list whatever FEARS may have led you to do what you did at the time.

- Now do a similar list for someone who you feel has hurt you and try to speculate on what their reasoning might have been for doing what they did. Think of how they may have also been acting out of FEAR.

- Go for a walk and look at other people you pass on your way. See them as CHILDREN. How does that change the way you feel about them and how you are affected by them?

- DO A FORGIVENESS RITUAL. Find 15 minutes in your day to take time out to do this ritual. Close your eyes and imagine that running from your navel are cords (like umbilical cords) that are keeping you attached to OLD and UNHELPFUL relationships. These relationships are attached to you by your hanging on to your HURT and ANGER – not only to OTHERS but towards YOURSELF. It is time to CUT THOSE CORDS.

Imagine a big sword is now coming down and severing those cords. Now see those people (and the person you were) drifting away over the horizon to their own destiny. Let them go in PEACE. They are no longer your CONCERN.

- Now think about what you have LEARNED from these encounters that you can use to IMPROVE your life from here on.

- Think of the times you feel that someone has been or is UNKIND to you. Ask yourself:

  When have I done the SAME?
  What is this person showing me about MYSELF?

- Finally, say 'THANK YOU' for this lesson.

YOUR
MANTRAS
FOR
DAY 24

'*People do things for their OWN reasons, including ME.*'

'*People show me MYSELF.*'

DAY 25

The HEART
of the
MATTER

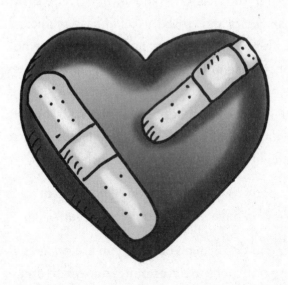

I'm now going to do the BIG REVEAL. Here is the reason you're depressed. There is NO OTHER REASON ...

... the ONE and ONLY reason people feel depressed is that they don't feel LOVED or LOVABLE and they are looking for love in all the WRONG PLACES.

Your sense of SELF-WORTH rests on YOU, but you place all the emphasis on SOMEONE ELSE'S behaviour or attitude towards you.

Do you BELIEVE you are WORTHY of love?

The BIG question is: do you love YOURSELF?

According to researcher and author Brené Brown, after six years and THOUSANDS of case studies researching the key factor governing those who have a strong sense of love and belonging in their lives and those who don't, it comes down to ONE THING: the BELIEF (or lack of) that one is WORTHY of love and belonging. NOTHING MORE THAN THIS determines one's ability to have loving relationships.

If you don't love yourself, you're going to attract people who have a similar opinion of you.

When you don't love yourself, you are endlessly looking to others to determine your worth and to VALIDATE you. But have you noticed that no matter HOW MANY TIMES others may tell you that you are

WORTHY or LOVABLE, it is NEVER enough? And what happens if others do NOT validate you in the way that you need? You fall APART.

You can give a million reasons why you might be depressed but at the heart of the condition is a feeling of being EXCLUDED, UNLOVED and UNWANTED, no matter whether this is in a corporate, recreational or domestic setting.

We all want to be loved. And if that's not coming into your life – whether it be in the form of a PROMOTION, a RELATIONSHIP, FITTING IN or myriad other situations – at the heart of this is a belief that you are UNWORTHY of these things. There is nothing more to your depression than this. This is the challenge that you must overcome. And it BEGINS and ENDS with YOU.

No-one else can do this for you. No-one else can fill the GAP in you but YOU. Stop EXPECTING them to.

Unless the relationship with yourself is SUPPORTIVE, KIND and LOVING, how can you expect others to treat you that way? It's just not going to happen. If you BETRAY yourself, ABANDON yourself, REJECT yourself and be UNKIND to yourself, why is it a SURPRISE if someone else does this to you, too?

If your NEEDS aren't being met – who is RESPONSIBLE for that? Is it someone ELSE'S job to ensure you're happy?

Should people behave only in a way that pleases YOU?

They won't. Give that up. Stop making OTHERS the SOURCE of your happiness or LACK OF. It's just not THEIR JOB.

The only thing you can control is your OWN wellbeing. This means learning to turn TO, instead of UPON, yourself, if the love you seek from others is not returned.

People MOVE ON, people CHANGE THEIR MINDS, or they simply weren't as INVESTED in you as you would hope. It doesn't mean they're BAD or WRONG. It doesn't mean you're BAD or WRONG. It simply means that they are not MEANT to be what you hoped they might be. And sometimes people DIE. Does that mean that your life must END, too?

If you can find SOLACE in being with YOURSELF, you will no longer need to look for it OUT THERE and find yourself settling for less than ideal relationships to fill the gap in yourself.

Today's work is focusing on having a healthier relationship with yourself, because this rubbish that you've been telling yourself for years – that you are UNWORTHY and UNACCEPTABLE – is RUINING YOUR LIFE!

Your self-loathing has to STOP. Nothing good can come from you hating yourself. You are a MAGNET. You are attracting to yourself the things that you believe you DESERVE. It's time to start DEMANDING only the BEST for yourself and believing that you are WORTHY of it. Just as you would want for someone you LOVE.

WORKING DAY 25

- Today, practise some SELF-COMPASSION. Imagine that a friend of yours was going through the same struggles as you. How would you COMFORT and SUPPORT him/her? Be KIND to yourself today.

- Contemplate this: have you made the significant choices in your life from a place of LOVE for yourself or a need to PLEASE or PLACATE others? How might you take better CARE of yourself in your future choices?

- Do some MIRROR WORK. Stand in front of the mirror and look into your eyes. See yourself now as someone who loves you would see you. Say something KIND to your reflection. Allow any feelings that stand in the way to come up for release. This is POWERFUL work. Do this each day. The ultimate aim is to be able to tell yourself 'I love you', with as much ease as when you say it to someone you care about. Today is a START.

YOUR MANTRA FOR DAY 25

'As well as I can, I will LOVE who I am.'

DAY 26

Self-
RESCUE

To help heal the relationship with yourself, you need to OWN the CHILD in you.

Deep inside each of us is a small CHILD. This INNER CHILD lives on, even when we assume ADULTHOOD, and this inner child is most active when we feel THREATENED, UNLOVED or UPSET.

Think about it: when you feel depressed and overwhelmed, are you really in your ADULT self?

This deep well of sadness that you feel – doesn't it trace back to when you were most VULNERABLE, OPEN and TRUSTING?

The depressed part of you is a lonely child who feels ABANDONED and unequipped to cope with the challenges of life.

This child wants someone – anyone – to ease the burden, to take the load and carry them through.

This child is crying out for LOVE from whomever will give it – it could be a PARENT, a BOSS, a COLLEAGUE or an AUTHORITY FIGURE.

The trouble with being a CHILD locked in an ADULT BODY is that no-one is coming along to heed the child's cries for help, other than in the form of a medico or therapist – and we wonder why we still feel so HELPLESS and HOPELESS, despite counselling sessions and medication.

Acknowledging that you are stuck in CHILD (and, let's be honest, CHILDISH) mode, where you want someone else to RESCUE, NURTURE and LOOK AFTER you, is the first step in some of the deepest healing you can do for yourself.

The next step is to embrace the fully present, capable and responsible ADULT version of you.

The final step is to be the one who RESCUES little you.

And you do this by assuming the role of NURTURING PARENT to yourself.

A NURTURING PARENT:

> *Understands*
> *Cares*
> *Supports*
> *Creates a sense of stability*
> *Gets things done*
> *Sets healthy limits*
> *Looks after you!*

Your role is now to be the source of LOVE and CARE for yourself that you had hoped OTHERS would be.

From now on, look only to yourself for the SOLACE and COMFORT you have been missing, and you can do this when you begin to see the CHILD in yourself as needing those things.

From here on, YOU need to be your OWN:

> *Cheer squad*
> *Decision-maker*
> *Caretaker*
> *Nurturer*
> *Best friend*

From here on, you need to CHAMPION your INNER CHILD.

No-one else can do this for you. But think of it this way – no-one else knows what you NEED, LIKE or KNOW as well as you do.

In the end, when you can fully TRUST and RELY on yourself, what others do will no longer be such a BIG DEAL.

You will have your BEST FRIEND walking with you – always on hand, always BELIEVING in you and SUPPORTING you. Isn't that worth pursuing?

WORKING DAY 26

- WITHOUT JUDGING YOURSELF, recognise that you're in CHILD MODE – especially when you're DEPRESSED.

- Also recognise that your inner child cannot feel COMPLETE unless the ADULT YOU looks after him/her.

- Take out a photo of yourself as a child and STUDY it. (If you don't have a photo, simply picture yourself as a young child.) Look at the little person that you were. See how you were:

    Innocent

    Open

    Trusting

    Playful

    Hopeful

    Vulnerable

    Small

    Deserving of all good things

Picture your INNER CHILD standing before you right now.

Is the child well cared-for or scruffy?

What is the attitude of the child towards you?

Is the child happy?

Now tell the child this:

'I've come back for you. I'm sorry I left you behind. I'm going to look after you so you feel safe from here on.'

Let your emotions around this surface. GRIEVE if you feel inclined to. Release all the HURT, SADNESS and UNEXPRESSED ANGER that has been trapped in the child you were.

- With your NON-DOMINANT hand (i.e. the hand you DON'T normally write with), have LITTLE YOU write you a letter telling how s/he feels.

YOUR MANTRA FOR DAY 26

'In the end, the only one who can STAND BY ME is ME.'

DAY 27

SNAP OUT
of IT –
why the
LONG FACE?

'A horse goes into a bar and the barman says ...'

Yes, I'm sure you've heard it – it's one of my favourite jokes.

Good grief, you've been taking life so SERIOUSLY, haven't you? What if you DIDN'T? What if you could instead LAUGH OFF life's ups and downs?

My dear, recently departed friend Paul often referred to life's pitfalls (or pratfalls!) as 'cream pies'. Just when you think you've got it all sussed, splat! Someone OFFENDS you? Cream pie. Your lover LEAVES you? Cream pie. You go BANKRUPT? Sure, that's one helluva big, old cream pie, but it's still a cream pie. What do people do when they get a cream pie in the face? They LAUGH. And WHY do they laugh? Because it's hard to take yourself SERIOUSLY when you're covered in cream pie.

Let's be brutally HONEST, now. Deep down you think being depressed is sort of darkly INTERESTING, don't you? There's a certain ROMANCE to all that NOBLE SUFFERING, isn't there?

This is not WHO YOU REALLY ARE!

This is not where you are MEANT to be!

You are not on this planet to SUFFER!

You could actually be having FUN!

Conventional thinking says that you should never tell someone with depression to 'Snap out of it'.

Well, WHY THE HELL NOT?

How ELSE are you going to MOVE ON? You DO need to snap out of it!

You have been HYPNOTISED into a dark, dreary dream and now it's time to WAKE UP!

Humans have this weird idea that if they just stay put, staring at the PROBLEM, the SOLUTION will somehow miraculously arrive at the door. IT WON'T! YOU must go and COLLECT it!

And you can start heading in that direction by FAKING it until you MAKE it.

Your BRAIN doesn't actually know the difference between REAL or FAKED emotion. Even if you're PRETENDING to be happy, making all the right noises and doing all those happy facial gestures, it responds accordingly and sends happy chemicals to the centres that need perking up. Do this often enough and it might even get the message that feeling better is NORMAL!

Today's the day that you *pretend* to be a HAPPIER PERSON.

It's a BIG challenge, I know, especially because in order to do so you're going to have to let go of a whole lot of LIMITING IDEAS, such as:

> *I'm never going to get any better*
>
> *Life is never going to get any better*
>
> *I'm stuck and I can't move forward*
>
> *Life is hard*
>
> *There is nothing to be happy about*
>
> *I don't deserve to be happy*

The world is not made to FIT you. You're going to need to do a bit of work to be a better fit FOR the world, instead of chafing against it.

Fitting into the world requires you to build the following qualities:

> *Resilience*
>
> *Emotional intelligence*
>
> *Living in the present*
>
> *Retaining focus*
>
> *Responding rather than reacting*
>
> *Seeing opportunities in every problem*
>
> *Learning from mistakes*
>
> *Accepting yourself and others*

Like it or not, you started this 30-Day project and today's challenge is possibly the BIGGEST one of them all. Are you up for it?

WORKING DAY 27

- Change your posture and STAND TALL. It's hard to feel EMPOWERED when you're slouching and collapsed.

- DRESS WELL. Today, have a bath or shower, wash your hair and put on neat, ironed, clean clothes. If you wear make-up, put some on; likewise, jewellery. Savour the feeling of freshness and the confidence of being well groomed. Take PRIDE in yourself. Imagine you are ROYALTY.

- SMILE. Your brain doesn't know the difference between a FAKE smile or a REAL smile! Even PRETENDING can lift your mood. Even better, recall a time when you found yourself laughing so hard you had TEARS streaming down your face and CRAMPS in your stomach. RELIVE it right now. Feel the laughter bubbling through you again.

- ENGAGE YOUR *HARA*. In martial arts, the *hara* is the seat of WARRIOR STRENGTH. When the *hara* is collapsed, you have no 'oomph'. Get it back by focusing on your solar plexus and sending energy to your *hara*. Notice how much more ROBUST you feel now.

- TELL A JOKE. You can borrow the horse joke if you like!

- See how many situations you can turn into CREAM PIES instead of hardships.

YOUR MANTRAS FOR DAY 27

'Today I'm trying on a HAPPIER and more DIGNIFIED version of myself.'

'I will LAUGH at life a little more.'

'Life is full of big, old CREAM PIES.'

DAY 28

The only way
is UP

While you might now be more WILLING and RESOLVED to finally make the climb back from all that sadness (good on you!), the DISTANCE from the bottom of the hole to the top might still seem a little daunting.

As mentioned previously, even though being depressed feels HORRIBLE, it has become familiar, and feeling some degree of BAD may be all you've known.

Anyway, feeling bad can become a HABIT, and habits can seem notoriously hard to break (just ask anyone who is trying to quit smoking).

From the bottom of the hole, the climb may seem too STEEP, too HARD and too SCARY, involving precarious grasps at slippery walls.

That's why I'm now giving you a LADDER!

Let's call it the 'Ladder of Emotional Ascension', and this is what it looks like from TOP to BOTTOM:

1. Joy/empowerment/freedom/love/appreciation
2. Passion
3. Enthusiasm/eagerness
4. Contentment/acceptance
5. Optimism/positive expectation
6. Hopefulness

7. Doubt

8. Pessimism

9. Worry

10. Disillusionment

11. Blame

12. Anger

13. Desire for revenge

14. Hatred/rage

15. Guilt/unworthiness

16. Depression/despair/powerlessness

Each of these emotional states represents a RUNG on the ladder and, clearly, DEPRESSION is as low as you can go.

Unless you've experienced some amazing EPIPHANY while working your way through the 30 Days (wouldn't that be GREAT?), so far, it will be a STRETCH for you to leap straight from DESPAIR to unbridled JOY. But it is entirely possible for you to work your way progressively to the top by stepping onto the NEXT EMOTIONAL RUNG.

Simply put, any of the rungs is a step UP from rock bottom!

For example, allowing yourself to feel anger means that you have ENERGISED yourself out of the NUMBNESS of depression.

While emotions such as ANGER, thoughts of REVENGE and BLAME are not IDEAL states, they are a way of moving out of the 'coma' of depression.

Besides, you're not meant to STAY on any of the rungs! The idea is to keep CLIMBING up them, step by step, and, in doing so, FEEL your way to wellbeing.

Ready to CLIMB?

Then let's GO!

WORKING DAY 28

- Climbing up the emotional ladder involves taking ONE RUNG at a time.

  Since your THOUGHTS determine how you FEEL, it is your thoughts that will take you from one emotional state to the next.

  On the lower RUNGS, you are simply aiming for one slightly LESS NEGATIVE thought to move you upwards.

  Towards the MIDDLE, you are in more or less NEUTRAL territory.

  The HIGHER RUNGS have you feeling BETTER and BETTER.

  You can tell whether you have moved up by the way you FEEL. Notice when you feel a little BETTER.

- Pick ONE SITUATION that you feel DEPRESSED about, for example:

  'My partner left me for another woman.'

- Now move on to GUILT/UNWORTHINESS, for example:

  'Obviously, she is more attractive and interesting than I will ever be.'

- Next, HATRED/RAGE, for example:

  'I hate him for what he did to me!'

- Now, DESIRE FOR REVENGE, for example:

  'I hope she dumps him!'

- Next, ANGER, for example:

  'I am so angry with him!'

- And now, BLAME:

  'He was always selfish!'

  Let's explore a bit HIGHER up now, so you get the PICTURE.

- PESSIMISM, for example:

  'I'll never find a love like that again.'

- Now, slightly higher up, to CONTENTMENT/ ACCEPTANCE, for example:

  'I have the freedom to do what I like, when I like.'

  And so on, as HIGH as you can go.

  Make a copy of the list of steps on the ladder and use it anytime you feel your mood slipping.

The author wishes to acknowledge The Emotional Scale exercise as the original version of this concept, first developed by Abraham-Hicks. This is a modified version.

YOUR MANTRA FOR DAY 28

'The TOP is in sight, when I stop looking DOWN!'

DAY 29

STORY
time

What's your STORY been till now?

We all live to our STORY and let it DEFINE us. Our story determines:

> What we think we are capable of
> What we think we deserve
> Whether or not we are capable of certain skills
> Whether or not we are worthy, lovable, successful or popular

To get a handle on the type of story you have embraced through DEPRESSION, think in terms of concepts starting with 'I am', such as:

> I am DEPRESSED
> I am WOUNDED
> I am UNLOVED and UNLOVABLE
> I am LOST
> I am STUCK
> I am a BURDEN
> I am HOPELESS at _____

Sometimes these 'stories' extend into the FUTURE, such as:

> *I will never find HAPPINESS*
> *I will always be ALONE*
> *I will never GET OVER THAT LOSS*
> *I will never FORGIVE that person*

The trouble with stories is that we build our LIVES around them. You tell a story in your HEAD, then make everything FIT the story!

And to make everything fit your story, you need to EDIT OUT anything that DOESN'T fit. If your story is built on the examples above that means cutting out anything that even vaguely resembles PLEASURE or ENJOYMENT! This editing process means that you turn a happy event on its head and focus only on things that CONFIRM your story, such as things that did go WRONG or even things that COULD go wrong (before they've even HAPPENED)!

This editing process even works retroactively, because your story is built on certain 'facts'; if it is a story of past STRUGGLE, TRAUMA or HARDSHIP, then you will have edited out any past happy events or successes that CONTRADICT the story.

Today is the day to decide to tell a NEW story – one that SUPPORTS and UPLIFTS you. It's time to THROW OFF that old version of who you are and write a new version that invites in more:

Acceptance

Approval

Appreciation

Pleasure

Contentment

Enjoyment

Optimism

Self-belief

Self-nurture

Forgiveness

Hope

Sound like a FAIRYTALE? Well, it's no more FICTION than the story that tells you you're UNWORTHY, that EVERYTHING'S HOPELESS and that there's nothing to LOOK FORWARD TO, because that's simply NOT TRUE.

And it's time you stopped BELIEVING in it.

Tell it how you WANT it to be, LIVE it how you WANT it to be and IT WILL BE!

WORKING DAY 29

- Today, you're going to construct your NEW STORY about yourself and your life. In doing so, phrase it in the THIRD person, instead of FIRST PERSON (e.g. *'You are'* instead of *'I am'*).

  The reason for this is that the mind is more receptive to what it thinks are 'external encouragements', whereas first-person statements tend to bring up DOUBTS. Remember, you are telling the story as you would LIKE IT TO BE!

- Begin with your CHARACTER. List your good qualities (yes, you DO have them!) or qualities you would like to develop. Phrase these like this:

  You are _____ (for example):

  Kind

  Fun

  Strong

  Worthy

- Now list the things you are (or would like to become) GOOD at:

    You are good at _____ (for example):

    Swimming
    Cooking
    Being kind to animals

- Now add the things you want to be doing more of from here on:

    You are going to _____ (for example):

    Go to a movie or a gallery twice a month
    Exercise regularly
    Get on top of your finances
    Learn a new skill
    Meet new people

You can put ANYTHING you like into your story. Why HOLD BACK?

Now get it in your HEAD and make everything FIT your NEW story, just like you made everything fit the OLD one!

YOUR
MANTRA
FOR
DAY 29

*'Life is only that which fits the STORY
I tell myself about life.'*

DAY 30

HOPE
springs
ETERNAL

The poet Emily Dickinson said that hope inspires the GOOD to REVEAL itself. In other words, when you look for the GOOD, you will see that good was always there but had simply been hidden from your view by your own lack of BELIEF in it.

Without HOPE, the struggle goes on. Hope is crucial in giving us INCENTIVE. It provides us with a GOAL and something to LOOK FORWARD to.

Even having the HOPE of HOPE can lift you out of despair.

Until now, you probably felt that there was no hope because there APPEARED to be none when you had those depression blinkers on. But the truth is there is ALWAYS hope.

If I could tell you with confidence that I've seen your future and everything works out well and all you have to do is BELIEVE it will for that to happen, would you DO SO? Well, I'm ASKING you to now.

Hope requires an INVESTMENT. You can't see the final OUTCOME, but if you keep putting in a little hope for a better outcome every day, it must ACCUMULATE.

Hope is an investment in the idea that there must be something BETTER than this – and, of course, there IS.

Everything changes; nothing remains STATIC, so you can pin your hope on the fact that whatever emotional place you are in or have been in, you will be somewhere ELSE in time. And, if you have been committed to the work in this book, you will now understand that you have some SAY in what comes next.

Believe there is HOPE and you'll see it. Continue to DENY it and it will continue to elude you. Which do you CHOOSE?

Hope is the FIRST and LAST step on the way back to wholeness.

The idea of FAITH comes into play here – even if you have doubts about any form of Higher Power.

You can have faith that the sun will RISE tomorrow, or that a loyal friend will remain TRUE, or that your pet dog will LOVE you no matter what you do.

If you are open to the idea of a Higher Power, you may have often felt in this journey that you have been ABANDONED by God.

But when it comes to the concept of God or a Higher Power, we humans make one big mistake – we give him/her/it HUMAN qualities. God doesn't ABANDON, *we* abandon God, or cut ourselves off from a NATURAL FLOW, by insisting that things should be a CERTAIN WAY and feeling upset when they are OTHERWISE.

But, let's face it: we humans aren't really doing a great job of doing it the HUMAN way. It takes INFINITE INTELLIGENCE to create worlds. Maybe it knows better than us what it's doing.

Maybe he/she/it has a smarter way of getting things done if we would just allow him/her/it to get ON with it.

There is a saying: 'Let go and let God'. There's a lot of wisdom in stepping back and allowing things to unfold in any number of ways.

Expect the BEST and you're likely to see it. Sometimes this is quite, well, MIRACULOUS. But you won't see it if you insist on a pessimistic view because it won't match with your expectations.

Grab on to hope and NEVER LET IT GO. You have been through the WORST. Now hope for and expect the BEST.

WORKING DAY 30

- Today, 'get out of your own way' and be open to OTHER POSSIBILITIES. Step aside and watch as things unfold in their OWN way. There are MANY possibilities beyond what you have thought of!

- How might you embrace the concept of 'Let go and let God' today? (Substitute any other concept of a Higher Power or Natural Force if you are uncomfortable with the idea of God.)

- What if you stopped being so insistent on a future full of PAIN and embraced the idea of something BETTER? How might that affect how you feel RIGHT NOW?

- Find your PURPOSE. Set yourself some explicit goals with realistic, doable deadlines. Now list a series of small steps to get to your goal. Make a promise to yourself to ACHIEVE the goal.

- And finally, find something to BELIEVE IN. Yourself is a good place to start.

YOUR
MANTRA
FOR
DAY 30

'There is ALWAYS hope.
I just lost sight of it for a while.'

And so our work is done. I now say 'Namaste', which means 'The Pete in me salutes the Pete in you'.

And, for Pete's sake, have more FUN!

Also by
Bev Aisbett ...

30 DAYS 30 WAYS
TO OVERCOME ANXIETY

From Bev Aisbett, Australia's bestselling anxiety
expert and author of the classic national bestseller
Living with IT, comes a proven and practical workbook
to help people manage their anxiety, with simple
daily strategies for work and for home.

Based on the exercises Bev has been teaching
and writing about for the past twenty years,
30 Days 30 Ways to Overcome Anxiety provides
clear, simple daily building blocks to help people
manage their anxiety and assist in recovery.

Designed to be carried in handbags or backpacks
as a daily companion, this is a highly approachable,
concise, practical and, above all, proven method
of overcoming anxiety.

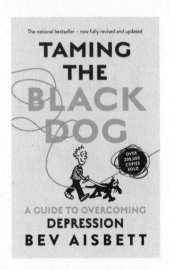

TAMING THE BLACK DOG:
A Guide to Overcoming Depression

Don't want to get out of bed in the morning?

Feeling as though the light is fading at
the end of the tunnel?

You may be suffering from depression, a condition
Winston Churchill referred to as the 'Black Dog'.

Now expanded and fully updated, *Taming the Black
Dog* is a simple guide to managing depression, which
an estimated 1 in 5 people will suffer in one form or
another at some time in their lives. Modelled on
Bev Aisbett's successful *Living with IT*, *Taming the
Black Dog* has a unique blend of wit and information,
and is an invaluable guide for both chronic sufferers
of depression as well as anyone with a
fit of 'the blues'.

LIVING WITH IT:
A Survivor's Guide to Panic Attacks

Panic attacks — approximately 5% of the population will experience them at sometime or another. Seemingly coming from nowhere, the dread of having an attack itself transforms the ordinary world of everyday life into a nightmare of anxiety and suffering.

In this refreshing and accessible guide, Bev Aisbett, a survivor herself of Panic Syndrome, tells us how panic disorders develop and how to recognise the symptoms. With the aid of her inimitable cartoons, she covers topics such as changing negative thought patterns, seeking professional help and, ultimately, learning skills for recovery. *Living With IT* provides much needed reassurance and support, leading the way out of the maze of panic with humour and the insight of first-hand experience.

FIXING IT

THE COMPLETE
SURVIVOR'S GUIDE TO
ANXIETY-FREE LIVING

Bev Aisbett

FIXING IT:
The Complete Survivor's Guide to
Anxiety-Free Living

What's your IT?

Anger? Fear? Low self-esteem?
Depression? Addiction?

Fixing IT brings together, for the first time in one volume,
a complete guide to surviving anxiety in its many forms
and how to move on to achieve change and growth in our
lives. This single edition includes three titles:

Living with IT: A Survivor's Guide to Panic Attacks
Living IT Up: The Advanced Survivor's
Guide to Anxiety-Free Living
Letting IT Go: Attaining Awareness out of Adversity